HEART TO HAND

An Enlightenment for the Mind, Body and Soul

MARGARET SELBY

BALBOA PRESS
A DIVISION OF HAY HOUSE

Copyright © 2016 Margaret Selby.

All rights reserved. No part of this book may be used or reproduced by any means, graphic, electronic, or mechanical, including photocopying, recording, taping or by any information storage retrieval system without the written permission of the author except in the case of brief quotations embodied in critical articles and reviews.

Cover Graphics/Art Credit: Greg Meyer

Balboa Press books may be ordered through booksellers or by contacting:

Balboa Press
A Division of Hay House
1663 Liberty Drive
Bloomington, IN 47403
www.balboapress.com
1 (877) 407-4847

Because of the dynamic nature of the Internet, any web addresses or links contained in this book may have changed since publication and may no longer be valid. The views expressed in this work are solely those of the author and do not necessarily reflect the views of the publisher, and the publisher hereby disclaims any responsibility for them.

The author of this book does not dispense medical advice or prescribe the use of any technique as a form of treatment for physical, emotional, or medical problems without the advice of a physician, either directly or indirectly. The intent of the author is only to offer information of a general nature to help you in your quest for emotional and spiritual well-being. In the event you use any of the information in this book for yourself, which is your constitutional right, the author and the publisher assume no responsibility for your actions.

Any people depicted in stock imagery provided by Thinkstock are models, and such images are being used for illustrative purposes only.
Certain stock imagery © Thinkstock.

Print information available on the last page.

ISBN: 978-1-5043-5920-7 (sc)
ISBN: 978-1-5043-5921-4 (hc)
ISBN: 978-1-5043-5950-4 (e)

Library of Congress Control Number: 2016908823

Balboa Press rev. date: 06/21/2016

CONTENTS

DEDICATION ix
FOREWORD xi
EDITOR'S NOTE xv
PREFACE xix
INTRODUCTION xxi

THE ENERGY OF SPIRIT 1
    Vibration 2
    Goodness and Grace 7
    Character 12
    Spirit Wisdom 17
    Miracles 20

MESSAGES ALL AROUND US 28
    Invisible Help 29
    Holding the Light 35
    Hearing Messages 43

GOD'S SOLDIERS 49
    God's Soldiers 50
    Soldier of Patience 54
    Soldier of Peace 60
    Soldier of Kindness 67
    Soldier of Compassion 73
    Soldier of Love 81
    Soldier of Grace 85

THE SPIRITUAL DYNAMICS OF PHYSICAL HEALTH ... 90
- Know Thyself ... 91
- Heal Thyself ... 97
- Effects of Using Your Free Will for Goodness ... 101
- Restful Solutions ... 106
- Doubts and Worries ... 109

SOUL GROWTH LIFE AFTER LIFE ... 114
- Chronology of Life Lessons and the Birth of Prodigies ... 115
- Divine Intervention ... 121
- Return to Earth Transitions ... 127
- Memories of Reincarnation ... 132
- Transgender, Gay, and Lesbian Genre ... 137

THE GIFT OF DISABILITIES AND DISEASE ... 143
- Cancer ... 144
- Children of Cancer ... 150
- Down syndrome ... 157
- Alzheimer's Disease ... 163

PHYSICAL AND SPIRITUAL SENSES ... 167
- The Basic Senses ... 168
  - Sight ... 169
  - Touch ... 173
  - Hearing ... 177
  - Smell and Taste ... 180
- Spiritual Senses ... 186
  - Origin ... 193
  - Growth ... 194
  - Assistance ... 197

IMPROVING HABITS 199
    Love of Self 200
    Attitude 206
    Rituals 209
    Fear 216
    Anger 221
    Wars 229

TENDING EARTH 234
    Realistic Expectations 235
    Heal Your Earth 241
    Wonders of the World 246
    Human Connections to the Animal Kingdom 249
    Earth Transitions 253

IN CONCLUSION 256
    Looking Ahead 257
    Living Your Moments 261
    Mindfulness and Managing Karma 267

PETER'S RECOMMENDATIONS 274
    Morning Stretch 274
    Morning Light From Heaven 275
    Morning Gratitude 276
    Meditation 276
    Breathing 277
    Sitting In Silence 277
    Contacting Guides 278
    Looking For Messages 278
    Listening For Messages 279
    Rituals 279
    Overcoming Fear 280

Preventing Anger 280
Prayer 281
Helping Tired Eyes 282
Heightening the Five Spiritual Body Senses 282
Affirmations 283
Helping Strangers 283
Body Scan 284
Love of Self 284
Attitude 285
Healing Thyself 285

PETER'S EPILOGUE 287
ABOUT THE AUTHOR 289

DEDICATION

This book is especially dedicated to two extraordinary friends. Shirlee Ryno, my angelic helper, was so instrumental for me to take chances and move forward to reach the path I am on today. Mary Jones has always believed in my work and offered encouragement to trust my writing and not look back. These two women have filled my heart with love and joy as I have followed their advice; I honor the ongoing spiritual sisterhood I embrace with them daily.

I also want to acknowledge the beautiful work of Peter and the many non-physical beings, and say "thank you" for being the one to bring this book from their heart to your hands.

Cover photo taken at Canyon de Chelly, AZ
Greg Meyer, Photographer and MD(H)
Board Certified in Internal Medicine, Urgent Care, and Classical Homeopathy
http://meyerhomeopathy.com

FOREWORD

Margaret Selby is one of the most amazing people that I have had the good fortune to know and love. It is hard to believe we met over 23 years now! She has been a co-worker, a dear friend, a Feng Shui consultant, a mentor, a spiritual guide, and someone who has stood by my side during the hardest time in my life, going above and beyond what anyone would have thought possible.

Margaret is such a strong, loving spirit who, with her infectious laugh and strong southern accent, can be totally disarming when she starts to tell it like it is, giving profound life-changing messages and information in such a direct manner. So I was absolutely thrilled to hear she had completed this work and was very honored that she asked me to write the forward to it. This book is, simply put, an extension of Margaret's brilliance.

When I first received *Heart to Hand*, I felt a very strong energy of love and peace, and knew within the first few pages that this book was like no other. The messages and stories are life-transforming, giving us insights into the world unseen yet often felt. We have been gifted knowledge and greater understanding through the channeled messages Margaret has been blessed to receive on humanity's behalf.

Heart to Hand has so much to offer! The combination of Margaret's real life stories from intuitive readings she's conducted over 25 years and the deep and meaningful messages from Peter and the collective group of souls channeling them makes this material incredibly powerful. It gives the reader a sense of peace knowing that there are benevolent forces constantly with us, rooting for us and willing to help at any time. It opens up the mind to the possibilities of connecting to our guides and angels, and being able to draw on the powerful love, joy, and energy from the other side.

It also gives us tangible exercises that we can apply to our lives on a daily basis to create habits and rituals that strengthen our spiritual growth and connection. The world is changing at an accelerated pace and it is so easy to feel overwhelmed, stressed, frustrated, worried, and many other negative emotions that rob us of our joy. But knowing that we are not alone, and that we can tap into these loving energies, will heighten our ability to reach our full potential.

Even with challenges and illnesses, there are always lessons for us on a soul level. Living a purposeful life is one of the biggest gifts and THE path to spiritual development. This book is a powerful tool for each and every one of us to support our journey.

The emphasis on joy, compassion, kindness, and love for oneself and for others will help to raise our personal energetic vibrations and collectively this is what the world needs now to heal. So yes, even one person CAN make a difference! It's essential to take that personal responsibility knowing that it will have a meaningful impact.

Enjoy the readings; savor the pages and the deep spiritual wisdom you will gain from these wonderful teachings.

Come back to them often and be guided as you open your own abilities to tune into the loving entities and powers that stand behind us. We are blessed that Margaret has been an open channel to receiving this wisdom for us all and is now sharing these incredible messages with the world!

Karin Volo
Chief Joy Bringer
Co-Founder of Evoloshen Academy
Author of International Bestselling *Engage!* and *1,352 Days*
http://karinvolo.com

EDITOR'S NOTE

This momentous body of work comes at a time when people are well poised to receive it, starved as we are for a better way of living and sincere in our search to make things better – for ourselves, sure, but even more for this beautiful energy system we call Earth and all that exists naturally within her.

It has been a complete honor and pleasure to edit this book for Margaret. And fun, to preserve the voice within both her stories and within the writings from Peter and the non-physical beings. As much as their powerful and magnanimous message, I hope you enjoy their personalities as have I. While Margaret can deliver a sentence three pages long with perfect formation, there is some awkwardness in the non-physicals' discourse, and I did not eliminate all of that because in my opinion it is part of their charm and validates their unique perspective. I have only endeavored to see that their sentences reflect coherent language and carry some cohesion. The content itself is purely yours to interpret – where their meaning may be unclear, consider that perhaps some further readiness on your part may be required to understand the section in question. Over the past several months, I can say that such readiness has been at work for me.

I found myself personally changing immediately upon beginning to read this material, gentling shifting my perceptions, priorities, and pastimes. It's as if the information sifted its way into my… thinking? No, into my being. As with most personal development, these changes were at the same time subtle and profound. Like the sides of an angle, what may start as a small difference becomes greater and greater so that where you are down the road is vastly different from where you would have been without it.

For example, the first material I reviewed (which went to IN CONCLUSION: Looking Ahead) included the following:

> *There will not be a walk down the street or past a desk at work that this new life you will experience will not emit this lovely energy. Much will be broken down and new faces that you have passed by will now be upon you and be part of your life in goodness and grace.*

With no conscious effort, I noticed that I was taking in people's faces as they passed me – say, in a mall, at a gas station, waiting at a street corner for the light to change. I began remembering the individuality of passers-by several times longer than I would have before. Had I subconsciously told myself I wanted to do that, or was I actually receiving this kindness energy? It doesn't matter to me how it came about; I am grateful for the mindfulness. For someone else, "new faces" may mean aspects of others they had not been acknowledging, or different ways they start to express themself – the meaning really is for each person to interpret.

There cannot be an incorrect way to navigate this book, for while the chapters are organized around themes, each writing can be taken as a stand-alone message. Whether what catches your attention is the powerful nature of love, or the mechanics of how energy affects our physical bodies, or the deep influence of small of gestures, or the soul blessings to be found in disadvantages, or the resilience of the human spirit, or the ubiquitous support that constantly surrounds us – I hope you also find yourself personally changing in directions for which you've wanted a better understanding of how to proceed.

Joanne L. Gartner, PhD
Educator, Shamanic Practitioner, and Certified Clinical Hypnotherapist
Author of *Looking Under Things to Get Over Them: True accounts of subconscious inquiry*
http://www.soul-liberations.com

PREFACE

I am honored to be sitting in front of my computer telling you how this book came about. Being a psychic clairvoyant for much of my life has certainly taken me on many journeys of pure adventure and wonderful friendships that have bonded for this life and beyond. Not one encounter has been for naught, yet it has taken a lifetime to comprehend the power of each connection and see how these acquaintances have woven my life into what it is today.

We all get hunches, some of them come at times of chaos, and often we brush them off as crazy talk and let them go. Well, as a child, I thought I had a bunch of crazy talk going on all of the time. Then as I had other experiences, I began to understand I was not alone in my head. My childhood prepared my early 20's and 30's for communing with spirit on a regular basis through sight, word and thought. I truthfully knew there was more to this reality we live in than what we perceive on the surface, and so I guess you could say over the years this book was growing organically for when the time was right.

Late one evening a voice spoke to me with kindness and authority to pick up a pen and get a pad of paper, and *Heart to Hand* was born. Tired from the first 60 pages quickly written, I set it aside for bedtime not knowing what had just been gifted to me. When it came time to transcribe this material, I realized the beauty and wisdom I held in my hands was from my wonderful, astral friend Peter and other non-physical beings that have been chosen to share their energies of awareness and love with those who are looking for a journey of their own.

This is not my first rodeo with automatic writing from the spirit world. Besides helping other people, I have received messages for years that helped me find answers to my own questions regarding life on the other side; however, this is the first time I have been told to publish for the world. This work has been continuing for months and future words are still coming to be shared with you. I hope this material for which I am merely the vessel to deliver will grace you with a more opened mind and a desire to search in your heart for what can personally flow and resonate with you at this time in your life.

Everyone wants to know what lies ahead and today the world is opening secrets at record speed, elevating our spirits to seek information about higher level energies – information available to all who choose to embrace it. Holding this book in your hands is your subconscious mind nudging you to embrace the inner voice which we all have and which is flowering anew as we speak.

For personal readings from Margaret, call 828.312.4229 or use mjgselby@gmail.com

INTRODUCTION

As we all know, when we are ready to listen we will hear a voice – timing is everything and the times are upon us today. This world is yearning for information and confirmation that someone or something is taking the time to help us listen and hear. Many of us are looking for validation of another way of living and are willing to push through the static we may get regarding that desire. When *Heart to Hand* started coming into being, I was asked to bring it to the masses and here we are.

This book has been automatically written through me by a group of non-physical beings wanting to participate in a human-contact interaction, with my guide Peter leading the way. You can pick it up and read from front to back, read any chapter, or read the writings in any order. What we are being given is deep insight of how humanity is beginning to open to a different way of understanding the life we are currently living and how we can grow in every aspect of existence at this time.

I look back and realize I have wrestled with quite a few of the topics these generous and loving beings discuss; thank goodness I have found my way successfully with their guidance. Doubts and worries together made for one of my biggest mountains to climb and it is one of the first topics they chose to give me. Yes, these troubles can lead to fear and stop you from learning who your true self is.

During that time I was having such aches and pains; something was always going on with my health. Every single time I chose to doubt and worry, creating fear, I was stopping my progress and living a very uncomfortable life. It certainly took some time for me to get it, stubborn as I could be, yet these wonderful beings were very patient with me. And the minute I got it, I was celebrating less pain than ever before – this new information changed my life.

Now my daily awareness of this issue is right up there with eating, believe or not. Every time I start to spend time in doubt and worry, I know I can walk right through that invisible curtain of fear I am creating and go to silence and stillness to release it. This is my biggest reason for bringing *Heart to Hand* to you just now. Doubt and worry can literally rob you of your spiritual birthright to develop your soul.

It is also my greatest pleasure to share with you true accounts, all anonymous, of people I have given psychic readings to that show you how the topics here play out in everyday life; you will find those italicized so you can clearly distinguish them from the information Peter and his friends are imparting. As this book proceeded, I was astounded to remember so many stories that so precisely fit the lesson being presented, no doubt assisted by the non-physicals there as well!

The introduction to each chapter takes information word-for-word from the writings you will find in that section. This gives you a clear idea of what you will learn there and does not risk skewing any meaning the non-physicals intended by paraphrasing. The intent of this book is to deliver their message in as pure a form as possible so, yes, you can expect to encounter those sentences again, embedded in deeper contexts.

Much of this book covers issues that we all have an interest in, although we are living them without much understanding of how they really operate in our lives. Here we are being given valuable information about our physical, mental, and spiritual health, descriptions of what we have to do to live longer, and how to feel better doing it. Of particular interest is their discussion of God's Soldiers, in specific writings and woven throughout other chapters. These are great souls, both embodied in physical form and operating from the non-physical side to help us all strengthen their namesake virtues – Soldier of Peace, Soldier of Love, Soldier of Kindness, Soldier of Compassion, Soldier of Grace, and Soldier of Patience. God's Soldiers are here in increasing numbers at this time, as the times are upon us.

THE ENERGY OF SPIRIT

Now is the season for the world to move to a new understanding of change affecting all mankind. The path the world finds itself on at this time is one of great disconnect, avoiding the oneness that is so needed for man to take responsibility to create love and acceptance. We are here to enlighten you on the desires of the spirit world to begin to connect on a daily basis. Be it understood, we are permanent communicators to your universe and will offer a window of wisdom that is available at any time you decide to be in stillness, to assist you in your life's journey.

Earth is a beautiful canvas for every soul to be the artist of everything currently emitting energy at this time; use your emotions to create a mindful picture of what you want the world you reside in to look like. There are many angels walking on your Earth at this time to give assistance to all humans and creatures. It shall be known they are God's hands and eyes when needed, granting many miracles that are not ever seen by your eyes or felt by your body.

You are born with a profound energy that will show itself to you at precisely the correct moments in time. It is our power to help

promote the love of giving yourself; the light of the masses is for all to partake. Every soul will participate in a miracle during their life span, which may come in any size and will occur under profound circumstances. It shall be up to you to choose at this time; you are in full control of your destiny.

Vibration

This writing reminds me of a psychic reading to do a full body scan for Gail, a teacher who was struggling with her desire to retire and heal her body. Feeling abused by the state budget cuts for education assistants and the subsequent overload of students in her classes, Gail was having pain that the medical field labeled as idiopathic and wanted to avoid the necessary medications to get through her day.

It certainly did not take very long for us to get to the bottom of Gail's issues – aside from insufficient sleep and pain, she lacked the vibration to handle the mental load she was carrying and was therefore attracting negative energies from the environment she lived in. She literally was feeding off of the low vibration that was creating a vortex around her every day when she opened that school door to her class. Negative thoughts fueled negative actions that brought on the pain and helpless feeling she was having.

Every issue Gail was carrying was a direct result of the negative thoughts and actions that were lingering from the classes held in her classroom all day. This was further escalated by the level of negative vibrations felt and projected by the other staff members dealing with the school's financial shortages and the extra burden on them for supplies needed to teach effectively. When we finished our reading, Gail began to see her new direction was right before her eyes when she looked around her classroom at the students' artistic abilities developing from their work in the art classes she was teaching after her regular workday was over!

I heard from Gail about four months later, just to tell me of the new adult classes she was teaching, as she knew I had an interest in learning to use watercolors in my own art. She said her pain was gone and her neck was better than new. "No more pains in the neck" she said, laughing as she was getting ready for an art show of her own work.

This is why the tools Peter has included in this writing for you are so valuable for everyone, regardless of your career situation and also to use for your home. Energy follows you, as you literally wear it by mentally thinking it. Sometimes we have to look at the big picture of what Spirit is trying to show us and where the happy point is to start from in our lives. Gail is a great art teacher and had the love to show others they could bring out their own gifts when it was their time to shine.

* * * * *

It is the season for the world to move to a new understanding of change affecting all mankind. It is not a dress rehearsal; it is a real change for all who are in the moment of need. The world has lost some of its ability to control the vibration required for a continuation of understanding at this time. Every human shall need to spend time moving into oneness upon retiring to your night of sleep.

This is a good opportunity to sit in stillness and breathe in the energy you need, holding for five seconds and then releasing. This will help the oxygen to clear from the body some of the particles of debris from the day. Sit and feel the lungs expand and enjoy the movement of release. In that very moment you are discharging the negative feelings that have been with you all day. It is time to let such energy go and not carry it to rest with your body, as it is toxic to the regeneration of your cells and their ability to operate in the correct manner. This practice will help you feel the body settle into a calm state for your rest. It is a very simple process for you and the benefits shall grow. This way you will enjoy a peaceful sleep, waking ready to fully participate in the new the day and raise your individual vibration to be a benefit for all.

Also know that taking the moments of uncertainty to bed with you is not for the health of your mind. Your world's frequency is being affected by so much uncertainty about what lies ahead. There is so much spoken, felt and feared by all of you at this time. Remember not to have those thoughts linger within, as they shall cause the problems we were speaking of earlier. All words, thoughts and fears that are released into the atmosphere, you are taking in. Should you weaken in any way, mentally or physically as you go through your day, make an effort to do a scan of your mind and body. This would be a good time for you to do your breathing exercises and remember to focus on what you are releasing from your body at this time. It is a time to become aware of the information that you receive back from energy vibrations which have been hidden from you humans on your Earth for some time.

Many know their time here is for goodness and have only touched the surface of this evolution for man at this time. We are speaking of future knowledge that should open for each of you when man's third eye opens on this Earth. Many are aware of this eye energy, and each soul has a very distinct time to find it. For all who have started the path of growth, regardless of age or experience, this will be your time to sync your mind and body in the physical temple you have chosen for the soul. This is the third eye to advance your own Earthly job.

Some of you have known since early in this life what you are here to experience. Some are picking up on their life plan when they meet their partner and others as they face tragedy. Sometimes tragedy comes to jolt the soul into the awareness of stillness in their life. This is to present them with silence so they may begin to know their strength and create determination. You ask, is this what each soul needs or what each soul has to do with a tragedy? The answer depends upon which lessons the soul has chosen for this turn. Determination is focus, just as it was when you were making your life plans in the afterlife. Upon this Earth that you know, it sometimes appears very difficult for some souls to bring determination into play. It shall be each one's free will to work it out either in this life or another.

Come into this place of peace and stillness; understand this shall be your opening to arrive to your own destination. It shall be up to you to choose at this time. There is much work being done on other energy levels by ones who are working directly with the psychic mental and emotional body of each human at this time. The excitement of humans embarking on change is related to this movement.

Your job shall be to do a scan of yourself every day, looking for any energy blocks you may feel at this time. Also it shall be necessary to slow down the amount of energy you are taking into your body if you are experiencing an excess of anxiety. If you are having any muscle or joint pain or tiredness, take a mindful scan of that area. Set aside some time to work that area either taking out the excess energy or massaging the joints to release the blocks you may have there. If your eyes are tired, burning or hazy, place warm compresses over them for three minutes, offering rest. Envision with your spiritual eye the cleaning of the debris you are experiencing. This will help you see more clearly what you need to focus on and move in that direction. You will see with greater purpose.

How you greet the day is your temperature for mindful ideas, work and spirit. It is a powerful action to soothe the muscles and put the cell energy to work at full speed, giving your mind the opportunity to feed the right information to achieve human desires. You should be mindful that you connect with similar energy vibrations – that is, if you are negative you will connect with negative, and positive with positive.

We emphasize various daily exercises that can be used to help you open to all that you should be evolving with, to your corresponding level. This loving energy can rise up and correct any and all unnecessary pain you may experience through any absorption of energy not fit for the body at this time.

Goodness and Grace

This writing reminds me of so many clients who are struggling at a crossroads based upon personal decisions hindered since childhood, and fighting self-acceptance. Among these are some who also have experienced much negativity from broken relationships; they lead the pack in the need for understanding to create a life of giving and receiving love.

I bring to you a reading for a young lady who came to me several years ago looking for help in finding direction to fill the empty space in her heart. Martha had grown up with a very dominant father who had spent his entire life in the armed services yet never accomplished the level of rank that he felt he deserved. His frustration played out in the form of verbal abuse within the family and a move every two to three years, setting the stage for Martha's search for her place of acceptance and the value of her mere existence. Both parents had passed by this time and although Martha stayed in touch with a sister living in another country, she felt she still had no one to call when she was in need of a friend.

One of the first subjects I approached was her lack of spirit to be part of something larger than her life today. She had literally placed her heart in a box and chosen to forget about it. It was hard for me to see how she was handling her inability to cultivate friendships. When I brought this up to her, she began tearing up and finally opened up to my vision, which indicated to me how powerfully Martha had shut herself down without anyone knowing her dilemma.

I spoke of her work not fulfilling her needs and that I felt a loss of employment was on its way since her company would be merging by the upcoming summer and her position would be eliminated. Asked if she was looking for other work, she was not sure what skills she had since her current job was simply setting up appointments for an insurance sales team and she still had one more semester to complete her degree. Martha did a good job and interfaced well with people on the phone, but it was her desire to get beyond this cubicle prison she called home during the day.

I could see it was absolutely imperative for her to work with people on a personal basis if she was to grow and overcome her life of strife. This was my chance to give her some encouragement to find a career that would fulfill her and provide the confidence she needed to break into a new line of work. She would flourish tenfold just by believing in herself and friends would miraculously appear. So I listed the dreams she had discussed, for her to connect with, and asked her to write down a wish list for her life going forward; we were to talk again in a week.

I didn't hear from Martha for about three weeks and wondered if she had chickened out on making changes *that would set her life on a path of peace and happiness, something she definitely needed. So I decided to make the call myself and was pleasantly surprised that she had followed my advice to find a counselor she connected with, but most of all her list was full of affirmations and using I AM discourses of God's presence in her words to receive His bounty. She was excited to feel her life changing ever so slowly, and knew it was the right path for herself. For the first time, Martha's list of things to achieve was getting shorter as she began to work through them, each one bringing her closer to a real life with love and friendships.*

Her low energy was improving as she smiled about starting her new job at a non-profit working with international charities. She had spent a week training with missionaries and the marketing team she would be working directly with. She shared how much the affirmations had helped her and she used each and every one of them daily – envisioning her new career, finishing school, making friends, and working for a local homeless shelter on Saturday mornings.

Martha called me a few months later to tell me more about how her life was changing; she was accepted for a position with the non-profit to travel on some overseas missions. The ability for her to help others and share her heart had put her on a path of understanding the bountiful amount of love she could spread around, inspiring others to find hope in their lives and promoting healing for all that came into contact with her. She has a ways to go in her new life, but her feet are well planted on the path to be a painter of light and help others fill their canvas with God's love.

What a blessing she has created for others lost on their way through the sheer bliss of her own journey.

* * * * *

The keys to the kingdom come from the heart and shall set you free from all obstacles that stand in your way at this time. You are in full control of your destiny to make choices to do good deeds for yourself and others. Remember the energy you express in your life shall come back to you. Every cell in your body gets a jumpstart from acts of goodness. It is a choice to change your life in ways to help your world so you may share what is planned for you and elevate the world's energy. Every conscious moment is a choice to expand your spirit and affect those around you.

Understand that each of you is at a crossroads in your life at all times, knowing there is always a choice to create great comfort for others when you see your world with kind, loving eyes. Know that you have the ability to partner with every soul you come in contact with on a daily basis to give of your heart; understanding this will serve you and the world around you. From such actions you will find a glorious Soldier of Grace who can assist you to comfort all people you meet and honor all events happening in your day. It is always best to give out your energy with a beautiful smile of acceptance and understanding for whatever shall be gifted to you in return.

There will always be days of frustration and slow understanding of the moment at hand for you, but that's no reason to issue a low vibration to another who does not have your same views. It will not serve any purpose to create a hardship for another soul. It should be known by all, only share what brings goodness and understanding with love from an open heart. Understand you are sharing a vibration that shall create a vortex for all energies of souls and objects around you at any time. It is your gift to this beautiful world to assist its vibrancy by allowing others to participate in the love and grace of the day.

All Soldiers of Grace come to assist you to handle your feelings with calmness and understanding and they will help you create an energy for dialogue with all creatures and humans alike, allowing them to honor another day in the life of each soul. Make an effort to understand your abilities and assist your world to grow and clean the energies that will raise all vibrations, giving and attaching only goodness to each other as you go about your day. If this can be understood and processed, it would create a kinder world for everyone, help remove illness as the body grows new cells every moment of every day, and promote the healing that can happen when all cells are in sync with the body's structure.

Should you choose not to participate in this way you are cutting the time for all humans to use this world and create a loving environment. We will speak quite a bit about the need to help this world with her vibration, as it is most important to remove negative energies that are holding back a spiritual world full of grace. Love is apparent in each soul and it sometimes gets side-tracked from lack of knowledge for what is being done without the composure of calmness and understanding that affects every living entity calling your world home.

Earth is a beautiful canvas for every soul to be the artist of everything currently emitting energy at this time. It shall be up to each of you to use your emotions as you daily paint to create a mindful picture of what you want the world you reside in to look like. This can mesh with others who are also creating their canvases of love and color, making it one masterpiece for all who want to envelop their bodies with this loving energy at this time.

Color has many emotions and it will become more evident for each of you as you mature spiritually, understanding this wonderful energy as you grow higher and still higher for all to be washed in its beauty. It shall be known that what each spiritual body brings to this world depends on their mindful participation. Many already see the colors of the world today as you prepare yourself for a more advanced level of love and vibration, colors that reflect the greatest beauty and brilliance of light known to man.

Character

This piece speaks to so many of my clients trying to find themselves and relinquish their feelings of not being worthy of relationships and love for themselves through a personal awakening of their own character. We are living in very difficult times as we are inundated with the need for picture-perfect bodies, attracting the ideal partner, and living a life of wealth. Looking for the perfect life and perfect mate can make it very hard to figure out our own uniqueness and the beauty we have been gifted with. Many will stay in relationships not suited for them or not feel worthy of love. Then they come to me feeling like their lives are spinning out of control and experiencing emotional turmoil that only reinforces their beliefs of unworthiness.

It's a tough road to introduce them to the life-path process. And a bit confusing for them to hear about the invisible connections they are not aware of and who can be of assistance just for the asking. Our non-physical helpers are always working through the energies to create a positive environment, offering help to us in understanding we are one. Here they use "character" as the buzz word, but it covers so much more than what I have talked about and deals with such important information – just about all of the issues held in our minds around loving and being loved.

This brings me to a call for a reading I had a few months ago. Anne was kind and very sweet, asking about a boyfriend who had backed away and moved out of her apartment. She was devastated, blaming herself for his actions. Knowing he was with another girl, her only questions seemed to be about his relationship with the new girl, whether she was pretty, if she was paying for stuff, and when he would leave her. Anne's voice was filled with anxiety yet there was also some light of assuredness; she could definitely wait for his return! She would work hard for money to pay his bills. Shortly Anne was gone just as quickly as she had come with what she wanted to hear, not what I said.

I cannot emphasize enough the great need to love yourself more than the one you are searching for. It takes time and you may find all kinds of reasons to not understand your own need to LOVE YOURSELF more than anything or anyone else. Asking for the courage of your higher source or God is the first step in developing your character. Honestly, I speak these words to many of you every single day and if I can only leave a small spark of energy flowing through your being from sound to thought, let it be this and I am happy.

* * * * *

Tonight is a new night and may we speak of welcome to the energy we have between us. Trust and love connections are in sync with the body of energy we all share in all worlds. This is oneness.

Character is something you just discussed with the one you were helping moments ago. Ah, yes, you can be the master of this help that is much needed for the troubled souls who come to you for comfort. The ability to feel peace and worthiness is character at its best for your teaching purposes. It is what we all strive for when we are trying to port ourselves to the high level of love and acceptance. Touch is so important to all creatures who call this planet home and man is finding the loss of this contact rapidly, creating a huge void. Through your words, people shall begin to experience thoughts of love and acceptance coming from all hearts equal as one from loved ones and peers.

The path the world finds itself on at this time is one of great disconnect and will continue to avoid the oneness that is so needed for man to take responsibility to create love and acceptance. This will take time to correct and shall be covered more at another time.

The body makes many changes that heal from inside to outside. Energy flows constantly and calmness sets in the rhythm of the cells healing. Love cannot work with only the brain and the voice. All connections need a clear electric charge to vibrate a level of worthiness. If you are a lonely cell and not attaching yourself to your sister and brother cells, you will die leaving empty pockets and the body will channel negative energy to fill the space. This may seem small, but please understand you have many millions of cells in the body and each is needed at all times for health. They have many jobs and interconnect with each other to be the premium task-masters they are meant to be.

Each cell is a mini-me of you with its own immune system, an internal mapping that is shared with all other cells. This operates much like your body does; it needs rest, nourishment, and interaction with other cells. Every cell needs the cooperation of its neighboring cells to work in tandem within the body to maintain the organs at a level of clean, pure energy for proper health. Not one cell is just for your brain or heart; they are all needed for the body to avoid disease and emotional stress.

Negative energy can consume the body and mind in a flash of time. People have this experience when they feel a loss of love from depression. Without the proper energy channels operating at full capacity, the brain and voice and heart cannot operate in a loving way that is needed to capture that feeling of good health and vibrancy. This you know when the body experiences a low in its desire simply to create motion you when you need to go forward.

Continue to talk of character to ones that need to feel they are worthy of love and acceptance from loved ones and peers. This is the track the world has created for a comfort zone and offers you a real connection with compassionate energy. We are projecting to the heavens and leave a track for all to move to. This is needed for man to understand the world they are living in at this time.

We are our own hunters and prey; this can be understood by the decisions that you make at this time. Look around and listen to all who will speak or pause to watch them. Everyone has a story they are not aware of themselves – walls are made and a Hollywood is placed in every city, small America and the world. Humans are acting out of pain, anger and false information, thinking a body and face of beauty is all that is needed. You cannot create a copycat life and expect it to work for the duration. This is the character many play by.

Time is of the essence for man to repent of his thoughts and actions. In the map of your life, if you do not make the change necessary to find love and be loved then you may create a false sense of security, certainly not a lasting one. You will not be following your true unique self that ports you to live your true path. This goes way beyond just love and your journey in life; you want to understand the inner voice that will help you know the twists and turns your life will take until it reaches its final destiny.

Animals are a good connection for all of us as they do not hold onto anger, just the distrust that is created through fear. Shall humans go into stillness and observe an animal in the wild, they will observe how it knows when to move on to what can serve it to integrate with mates, feed itself, anchor a place of rest, and raise its family. Revenge is a waste of energy; it is the same for animals and humans alike.

The light of the masses is for all to partake and use as much as you need to fill yourself up and give back out with each breath of the moment. It is our power to help promote the love of giving yourself without words of anger and war.

Spirit Wisdom

I love the way Peter is opening the door of wisdom that is at our feet every day for the taking. Many of us are just beginning to understand that in this game of life we are the ones holding the cards while our non-physical friends are the dealers. It is so magnificent to know we have teachers just for the asking and can be confident in the faith that they are with us at all times.

This brings me to an interesting psychic reading for Linda, who felt she'd had intuitive abilities to find her way through college and make decisions that took her into a very successful career in the world of technical support. However, the more successful she became, the less she understood her direction and believed she was losing her power to know and live who she really was. I foresaw her making a huge step in her career and that gave her some pause, as she had fear rise up in her gut that made her want to stop the discussion from going any further. Interestingly though, Linda's next question asked how a person can lose their connection to the universe and feel lost and left behind by guidance that was once so clear.

Actually we never lose our connection with Spirit and the non-physical beings operating in the after-life; sometimes we just choose another interest that steals our focus. When that happens, spiritual guides are very respectful of our choices, as we have that freedom within the contracts we have made for our present life. Many times, they are going to nudge you, but if you choose not to be in their presence, they will wait for your time. There is no force to awaken you; it is your free will.

This huge step showed up as her wake-up and she made the decision to return to her roots of inner knowing. She is now running her own media company and following her instinct to spend quiet time listening to the voices she has heard for most of her life. Linda happily admits she feels perfectly in touch again and feels the tickle on her hand that tells her she is never alone.

* * * * *

Today we are here to enlighten you on the desires of the spirit world to begin to connect on a daily basis. It shall not be a hard thing to do as you are already present in small increments as you think of us briefly. This is a whisper in your ear of our presence. We offer so much to you, almost like a ticker tape running all day long for you to pull information and guidance from at any time. Are we there each and every moment? Yes, we feel the need to assist you in your journey and prove you can draw from so many wonderful opportunities to interact which are flowing in the atmosphere just waiting for you. When you get a quick thought, train yourself to grab it instantly and assimilate the information. It shall be up to you to catch the feeling of its usefulness and put it to work.

We are giving the world information and some choose to take the ideas and transform them into powerful products or services. There is much to be said of your life changes that occur during these communications. The pearl of wisdom shall be available to each who has faith in its presence. We do not then leave you at such times; ask and you shall never be alone in your tasks. This can be done by setting aside time you would like us to communicate with you. Make this your daily ritual for your ideas to produce action on your part and become more tangible for you. You have to believe we are here for you to develop a relationship with us; it is our desire to offer help on a regular basis.

Should you desire to only communicate with us on a periodic basis, then sit quietly and call upon us for the time and subject you wish to address. Understand, we will answer questions for you in real time if you are making this time known to us in advance, as we are working with many on your Earth. This too shall help you to prepare yourself in setting aside time and know we will offer the help needed. This communication shall get better and better for you as you continue with us. Sitting quietly shall prove a proper connection and you will find you can be more productive as time goes on.

Be it understood, we are permanent communicators to your universe and will offer a window of wisdom that is available at any time you decide to be in stillness, to assist you in your life's journey. The words "I Am Listening" are your call of faith, adapting to changes put in place many seasons ago. When we speak of seasons, it shall be understood we are speaking of the previous lives you have experienced in any world you have chosen for growth or assistance with another soul group.

Miracles

I have always looked at miracles as new beginnings and over the years that analogy has proven to be so true. The reading I am about to share with you is spot-on for the writing Peter and his helpers have shared so gracefully.

This call was from Jennie, whose parents owned a small restaurant located in the Midwest. She wanted a special reading regarding her desire to get her parents to move to the West Coast. Specifically, she needed assistance in understanding why she was so adamant for them to move closer to her, which would require they close the family business. True, Jennie's, parents were getting older and needed to slow down and the business was doing well so it could be sold, but the restaurant menu was based on many of the family recipes from "the old country" which they guarded with their lives, as they had made a promise to her grandparents they would hand them down through the family and never sell them. She had a younger sister, Maureen who loved living in New York City and was not interested in moving to the Midwest to run her parents' Italian restaurant.

The first thing I saw was a bank and a stock market bell ringing, which of course seemed like a very strange vision for her parents' possible move. The next thing that I saw was an old box with a leather belt. The third image was a lot of wind; Jennie had spoken of the tornadoes that came through the area and felt it was noting her parents' home. I knew the move would take place in a few months and I felt the parents needed to get a value on the restaurant from a realtor, so we made an appointment to speak again after the appraisal and also to do a full reading with all of the family present.

I still couldn't get the thought of wind out of mind and I made a call to Jennie letting her know my concern. I asked if the restaurant had a storage area or a storm shelter and she said they did have one at both the house and restaurant. One thing I wanted her to ask her parents was where the recipes were kept and tell them they needed to get them to a shelter and bury them in some way. Jennie agreed to mention the recipes to her dad and then we would be talking in a week for the final reading.

A few days passed and I received a call early in the morning from the family to let me know of the tragedy they had experienced the night before. A storm had hit the area and had taken the restaurant completely down to the ground. Everyone survived but they were so upset because the dad had not yet moved the recipes to a safe place and they were now nowhere to be found. I told them everything would be okay, to look around the area; it just seemed to me that they would show up. I also felt the move was still going to happen, probably within the original timetable we discussed.

A few more days later Jennie called with news that was such a blessing for all of them; a real miracle had just been gifted to them, as the recipes were found several blocks away hanging in a tree from a leather belt, still in the box. And by the way, the box was an old cardboard one that her grandmother had placed the recipes in 30 years prior to handing them over! Her dad just couldn't believe they survived that storm as the box was worn from age.

Well, all was well and I felt they would be okay from that point on. The move would be in three months and they would settle into their new home on the West Coast. Jennie's husband was okay with her parents moving into a cottage they had in the back of their house, the more perfect because they had recently added a large patio that would serve well for cookouts. It was an ideal setup for big family gatherings and Maureen, the sister from New York, was coming out to help with the move.

While she was there visiting and helping them get settled, Maureen received a call to say her position would be eliminated within two months, as the financial institution was being sold, and it turned out she was not interested in making a move to another one. So it seemed my vision of the bank and the stock market bell was her part of the story, although she was not part of the reading. She became part *of the whole process once the discussion had turned to the recipes staying in the family. Since she had spent her young adult life in the family business, and she now had the funds as her stock had just hit an all-time high with the merger, Maureen decided to open a small restaurant in New York.*

Another two months passed and I received a call asking for my address; they had some barbeque sauce to send to me! The barbeque on the patio was used a lot and the whole family was getting into the process of making new recipes for a whole different menu. Needless to say, they are considering selling this one outright instead of starting a new business.

The New York restaurant is doing so well that Maureen received an offer from some investors to purchase it, but she decided to hang on to the family recipes, as they are the miracle. She has found a new husband and he has joined her preparing those recipes every day.

* * * * *

All souls' contracts contain miracles and every soul will participate in a miracle during their life span. There shall be some who have more than one miracle to participate in; they may come in any size and will occur under profound circumstances. Many of you may question the validity of giving or participating in a miracle for another human or creature of God. These miracles are like having a "Pass GO" for you to use when a difficult time is upon you. Understand it is not your purpose to wander around just looking to present a miracle to another human; it will happen when it's supposed to.

You are born with a profound energy that will show itself to you at precisely the correct moments in time. Some of these beautiful expansions of love are simply your words to help another person become aware of their beauty, love or kindness. Now you ask: how can a real miracle be only a few words of encouragement? Understand at such a time you may be helping that soul to be mindful of their real value and give a second thought to what may have triggered their own demise. They may only need your heart-felt words of comfort to have a moment of feeling loved, gain the strength to move forward, and return this beautiful pod of pure love and kindness to another soul. This, you are beginning to see tenfold in your world today.

Much of this type of action is coming from a younger group of souls newer to your Earth, who alone shall set their path toward goodness and love of themselves and others. This will be considered part of a new wave of mankind and it should become a normal activity for all humans to exchange feelings of love with one another. Even those who are strangers to you can benefit from your kindness and avoid negative actions, moving forward in grace and hence further spreading miracles throughout your world. The magnitude of these miracles would create an outlook that shall transform Earth into a state of love as they connect into one body of energy that multiplies rapidly for the betterment of all beings.

There are many miracles that seem to defy all reason of existence, such as a child being saved from a horrific accident, literally pushed out of harm's way by a miracle-giver and left totally unscathed by what otherwise they could not have survived. This is one of many kinds of miracles that are happening throughout your world as we speak. There will be more who appear saved by untold reasons and you may be thinking how lucky that person is at that moment to have survived, but understand it is also the miracle that was gifted to the ones who participated in the saving. They are certainly within their own divine moment of intervention.

This is a gift in itself and everyone will eventually have the beautiful opportunity to experience this lovely energy of pure light presented by your God to help another soul. It shall be left to individual souls to use this wondrous energy and love to assist others and begin a new life path for themselves in the inner knowing of their own grace. It can be life-changing if all souls choose to accept this "Pass GO" moment in life for the goodness of all mankind, bringing the energy flow to all corners of your Earth. Let there be no doubt that this effort is possible if people would only rise to their natural, advanced level of spiritual love. This can be set aside as it grows for a period of time until the soul is able to understand the value and magnitude of this precious gift God has bestowed.

There are many prayers requesting miracles for the health of loved ones who are ill and some may feel they were not heard by God; but it is just the opposite. Each and every prayer for another is heard and acted on based on the soul contracts. God hears all prayers and if a soul is terminally ill, it must be understood that their passing may be part of that soul's contract to leave this Earth at the proper time and so it is not appropriate to grant what you would consider a miracle for them. At such a time the miracle could be their leaving Earth and relieving the suffering of the family left behind. It should be understood that there are many souls who have chosen to leave this earth through illness or injury and prayers are still used for the transfer of ease for that souls passing.

Prayer is most valuable when the energy comes from those who are choosing to help someone heal the body of disease or broken structure. Prayer should never be overlooked as a miracle-in-the-making, as it does remind the masses of its value. Collectively, the power of prayer can create a pod of healing and elevate one's love to cleanse the body of the trauma and disease it may be carrying at that time. It also works on a cellular level throughout the body, not only for the person being prayed for, but also those who are doing the praying. When you pray to ask for God's assistance on behalf of another without any thoughts for yourself, you are feeling the energy of love that God is granting and you will also have a cellular healing. There is a higher level of pureness for any soul who chooses to assist another. Be it also understood, when you are praying before your evening retirement, it would be a blessing for you to always offer a prayer for your world of brothers, sisters, and creatures. This energy can be felt by all who are in need of a blessing.

There are many angels walking on your Earth at this time to give assistance to all humans and creatures. It shall be known they are God's hands and eyes when needed, granting many miracles that are not ever seen by your eyes or felt by your body. They are handpicked for this loving duty that they have been gifted with and use many times as a beacon of love and understanding with great power and benevolence for those who call Earth home. They are the helpers who appear in a dire time of need to carry you out of danger, and then leave when they are sure you are okay and in the hands of competent help. They are not to be seen so that their presence will change lives in magnificent ways and their gift of life will educate this world about the experience of true miracles.

Many of you may have had that same calling in another lifetime; it would be a beautiful gift to your world for you to practice this compassion and understanding for any soul or creature in need while you call this Earth your home. It is pure grace to have such love in your heart and hands.

MESSAGES ALL AROUND US

Invisible messages of glorious information are everywhere for all to receive as comfort as well as education; they can help any human willing to accept and trust at this time. It is just up to you to desire it and a make a decision to activate our help by being open to receive. It is not what you know; instead it is wanting to know.

Every soul experiences the gift of light at birth and death, and understands the absolute purity of its presence in oneness with God which shall be gifted in time when one has a desire to own this information. This light is of such purity that no breath is needed in its presence. Time is never too fast or too slow to see this beauty and feel it move from your heart to your hands, as it is of the moment for each to willingly participate through pure love and understanding.

Many are receiving this magnificent light and love from God to share with your world; it can reach the masses in a very short amount of time. There will be many spiritual helpers as you begin to develop the different levels of life lessons you are here to learn. Many messages go by unnoticed and at such a time Spirit will use another means for you to understand

and feel its presence. You are here to make a difference for yourself and others.

Invisible Help

I am sure you have had some of the same experiences as the clients I share with you in these psychic readings. We do hear what we want to hear at times and although we are constantly receiving information, we are used to hearing our own self, or so we think. Big ideas can be confusing yet pretty powerful when we get them coming through the pipeline of the universe.

The first client I will mention here was Bill, a longtime barber who had a great penchant for helping kids looking for a chance at a career making good money without a 4-year college degree. He s an interesting man who spent years 20 years as a military barber, then retired to a small family-owned barber shop, and had recently brought his son into the business thinking it was time to go fishing a little more often.

When Bill called he told me that, besides having a referral, he had to share his experience since our last reading together six months before. At that time he spoke of a voice that seemed to talk with him early in the mornings, sharing information about a random trip he should plan to a local prison. When he brought this up to me, I asked if he was receiving any additional information around the same time. He spoke of hearing the words "Be true to yourself." This message would come around at least once a week and usually when he was speaking to anyone he felt could use his great spiel about becoming a barber – how they could make a good living, meet a lot of people, and never be bored. Everybody needs a haircut, right?

I smiled when he had talked about his love of the business and how much joy he received from nudging youngsters into a good career so as to not end up in a hopeless position of having no work, like so many troubled kids who barely make it out of school with no way to get into college. While he spoke, I knew the message Bill was receiving was straight from the universe, opening the door to a new side job of teaching and mentoring disadvantaged youth. Furthermore, needless to say, he felt that might fit nicely with his son taking on some of his clients to lighten his work load.

Now he was so excited to share with me how it had played out, feeling he had found a new home for his talents. Bill had followed my advice and was volunteering with the state corrections facilities to mentor kids on probation in a certified state barber program that he had started. The referral he was calling about that day was Laura, a young lady who had spent some time in prison for DUI and drugs found in her car. He talked about having received a message to help some of the prisoners beyond his barber school and just wanted to give her a little departing gift a week after her mom had picked her up from the prison. This leads to the second client in this story.

When the call came in, I could hear Laura's mom, Carol, in the background recording the reading, not wanting Laura to miss any of it. I saw a box of old, broken watches laying by a dumpster at a watch repair store, and also some business cards with the name "Coming Home" on them. I asked if any of this made sense to her and it turned out Carol worked for the watch company and indeed had brought home the box of broken watches. The words "Coming Home" were part of the sign she made for her daughter's welcome home party. Laura had taken a class in metal sculpting and was interested in making jewelry so a new business began to take shape for this troubled young girl.

I spoke with Laura several months later and she indeed had started making jewelry out of broken watch pieces and old worn-out jewelry; her company was *Coming Home Brand New*. She was selling them well, getting into retail, and making a pretty good living. She was so grateful that her life had turned around and decided to start a charity, which she was directed to do by messages she was receiving. Laura had found her way because a generous barber got the message she was special enough to help out, the both of them understanding the power of hearing and acting on internal guidance without fear.

* * * * *

There are invisible messages of glorious information that abound on your Earth for all to receive as comfort as well as education; they can help any human willing to accept and trust at this time. These invisible messages make information available for the taking and are part of your growth and enlightenment. Having an inner voice that is constantly available to you is to live in the moment, listening to the inner questions you are processing at all times, hearing the answers, and acting on what is necessary.

There is a message born with every breath that is drawn in and released. Understand that from this wonderful ebb and flow of messages many will go by without any takers. We do not impose on any human to choose all the assistance that is placed in your energy field; we are only here to encourage mental mindfulness that you will be open to it at the time. Nor do we address what shall be used or let go, that is strictly your choice. Understand that being in the moment you can listen and receive the messages you are then to expand your own mind with. You may experience the messages as they flow into your moment of time without any knowledge or desire of where they came from, just to experience.

If you could view your brain as a ticker tape it would be miraculous to see how much data is being processed in every moment. The value is enormous for all beings and this data feeds your private storage of questions that your higher self is engaged in with your heavenly helpers at all times. These heavenly helpers are making the information available to you for the taking but unfortunately man has many blocks to hearing and using this magnificent knowledge that is being offered.

It is to be understood that the brain is constantly striving to open many of its unused cells to allow the incoming data to make connections you can use if needed or wanted at that very moment. Much of this information seems to be just mindful chatter to you. How many times have you been driving along in your car and said to yourself "I should change lanes now," but you chose not to act on this information and soon found yourself stuck in traffic. Then out loud you said "I should have made that lane change." That was when you were remembering, right?

Should anyone sit in stillness each day for a small amount of time, you would be able to calm your energy and open this pipeline to the cells of the brain for information to be processed and made useful to you. There are times when it might impart something that is unfamiliar to you and in passing you speak out loud "Where did that come from?" This is the time to say "thank you" to your heavenly helpers, as they have given you the opportunity to hear some of the data we are talking about that you are constantly receiving. You can receive a heavenly education on a subject that is embedded in your mind, something that you have unconsciously had an interest in at some point in time. Such an interest can also come from a quick peek into another lifetime, forward or past.

When in silence you can expect to feel emotions that are infused within the words. If there is a very strong emotion or a cycle of thoughts around the information, then you must act accordingly. It should be said that all messages have merit but they are only meant for you at that time. You may stop and listen for more and if that is all you receive, that is your meat for the day, your thoughts to ponder and should you feel the desire, then act upon them with certainty that you have received all you need for this time. The messages can be more than heard and felt; you may choose at that very moment of receiving to view something that comes to the eye, which may be a memory from your current life or a past life.

Many messages have very important information for you to understand, which at some times is very clear and other times appears to be cryptic. Some will offer you direction and love while others will pass ideas and direction. There is much heavenly guidance that is present to assist you in moving through your life path in a newfound way without fear, helping you to see ahead. You can have messages that offer caution of things coming ahead for you and it should be understood they are not always dire warnings of danger. This shall be the time to listen and should you have any feelings of distrust for a message, then stop and ask to have only the messenger of God's light in your presence with directions that shall be active for the highest and best use of your soul. And then really listen with undivided attention for the divine answer you will receive.

The messages will come to you to assist you with your emotions at your time of need, often with words of calmness, reflections on your own life, and small journeys where your thoughts take you. This should be understood as a teaching moment for any human to live in the moment. Without the balance of energy and calmness, no thoughts have meaning.

Many humans have fascinations with stones that are smooth and shiny. Usually you find them by water and they are just as alive as the message you are receiving. The message may be as simple as love for the moment you feel with the stone in your hand, embracing the energy it is bringing. This can take you back to a time when you felt the need to express a feeling that maybe was too strong to do so, and this new stone gives you now a feeling of beauty and sturdiness in your hand to help you adjust to that emotion at this time.

It is not our desire for you to pull into a memory bank each message and act on it later. Better to accept that these beautiful words are chosen for the exact moment of silence you are experiencing at that time – words to empower you right then and you will let go of what is not needed in that moment. Please know we and many others are messengers who are willing to help you understand the value of this mindful information; it is just up to you to desire it and make a decision to activate our help by being open to receive.

Holding the Light

There is so much power and love in this writing; I have a reading that so well applies to Peter and his friends' beautiful message here. I am grateful for the gift of my work and allowing me to share this very special experience I had the absolute honor to share as a psychic.

At first, the reading request seemed just a normal booking for Jennifer, in her 50's and trying to make the decision to have a facelift, wanting to talk about her fears and timing for the surgery. I could tell it was a very big deal for her, as she was newly widowed and feeling a need to turn the clock back a few years, excited but also a little nervous.

It started out pretty easy and then became rather teary for her as she explained the spiritual path she had recently started and wanted to ask some questions about her fear of the surgery, even though she felt it was absolutely necessary to go through with and wanted me to know that I was not to try to talk her out of her decision. I asked if she was worried about dying, as I saw a Bible that was set aside with a file of personal information on her desk. She also had penned some letters to her family and friends which were stacked on top of the file. She was shocked that I knew of this ritual she had just completed that afternoon before she called me.

Jennifer's marriage had produced no living children; she had lost a child early on and was never able to get pregnant after the miscarriage. This always bothered her, so her husband Grady, encouraged her to return to school for a teaching degree and she taught school for several years and loved it. However there were changes that would make it a love cut short; Grady was diagnosed with Parkinson's and as the disease was progressing, Jennifer decided to quit teaching to care for him. He lived several years and was house-bound, requiring round-the-clock attention. Beginning to feel she had become a prisoner in her own house, they hired Marian, an older woman to sit with him while she would go to mass every day and spend a few hours running errands. She became fast friends with Marian and as they would talk about her spiritual path, Jennifer decided to start her own journey of finding peace, fueled with knowledge of the impending loss of Grady's passing. She had learned much from this special lady and was beginning to prepare herself for the life changes ahead.

I saw Jennifer taking a trip to another country and standing on a balcony with several people that she appeared to know. Upon hearing this, she started to cry about wanting to take Grady's ashes to his native country of Costa Rica, since it was his dream to go there before he passed. Needless to say, he was too sick to make the trip and he'd made her promise she would visit and set him free on the beach. This was Jennifer's biggest fear, visiting a country where she knew no one, because she had never traveled enough to feel that was something she could do. I told her the trip would happen, that she would have a chance to choose someone to go with her, and although she said she had no one, I knew that would change.

We talked quite a bit about her fears. She wanted to tell me she felt she would see Grady again soon and that her biggest concern was that she would pass away during her procedure. Although she wanted to see him again, she just was not ready to go at this time. I told her he would be with her during this surgery and assured her she would be waking up probably in some pain but would be okay with her results from the operation.

Jennifer called me a few weeks after her surgery to tell me about the amazing experience she had had during the procedure. She spoke of feeling herself lift off the operating table and float away into a beautiful white light that she thought was at a distance and found herself embraced in a white light among family and friends. Grady appeared to tell her how much he loved her and another voice came into the room telling her she had more to do and she would be coming back to complete her work. She said she was so in awe of the presence of this being that she just drifted back into her body and Grady held her hand while she laid there and he was with her when she was moved to the recovery room. He told her she would be making the trip to Costa Rica and to take his caretaker, Marian, with her; he knew they had become close to over the past year of his life.

When Jennifer woke up from the surgery, she told the doctor of her story. He told her he too believed she had felt her husband's presence, as she had done so well in the surgery. And that since she had someone waiting to take her home, he was not going to keep her overnight. When she looked past the doctor to see who was there, it was Marian!

About five months passed and I heard from Jennifer again as she was leaving for the airport to return back from Costa Rica with Marian. They were already planning another trip there, as she had bought a condo and was looking to eventually move by fall or winter. Jennifer had laid Grady's ashes on the ocean front right outside the condo and told me how wonderful it was to feel like she was finally home, too. She had made some new friends and was looking to do volunteer work with a school there as well as find time to travel, since she and Marian made perfect travel buddies. I then heard from Jennifer again about a year later when she was working as a tour guide, traveling just the right amount of time. She had found a new man to share her life, a retired teacher, and decided to make the move permanent.

She told me Grady had left a letter in her Bible, which she had overlooked during her time of loss. As she was unpacking from her move, she was astounded when it fell out of the Bible along with the other letters she had previously written to her friends and family if she were to pass away during the surgery. Grady's letter told her to have a happy life, to follow her heart, and that if she found someone, it would be okay. He knew she would have no fears about making the right decision, said he would see her someday, and put a smiley face at the end where he told her not to hurry because he wasn't going anywhere. Jennifer was so happy to find that letter and feel the love she had had with him; she absolutely knew she would see him again.

She destroyed the other letters she found in the Bible that she had written to her friends and family, as she had no fear anymore, realizing when the time came that she would need to write such letters again, she would have a lot more positive and wonderful stories to tell them and thank them for being part of her new life to come.

* * * * *

Every soul experiences the gift of light at birth and death and understands the absolute purity of its presence in oneness with God which shall be gifted in time when one has a desire to own this information. This light is of such purity that no breath is needed in its presence. It holds the heart at such a high vibration that no adjustment shall be needed within your physical presence at the time of its gift.

God chooses to enlighten many with this light, as a time of message and an honor for a soul to receive this presence while in their current bodily incarnation.

Understand this is experienced by all beings on some level during their lives spent on your Earth or another world. This allows a human to catch a glimpse of the ominous presence of your God and those living in the afterlife. Many of these messages are given and remembered completely at the time of returning back to the human state of being on your Earth. There can also be an atonement for the soul to announce to your world, for this heavenly power that is pure love and whose greatness can never be completely explained to another human until the original state of being for this soul is restored.

This beautiful glimpse into the light of God comes at the correct time for each soul and is often attended by other souls who are partaking in the correct circumstances for this event to take place. It can happen when a human is receiving medical attention and the soul is not fully contained within the body. Understand the others present are only the vehicle for this event and are not aware of the process but are attuned to the condition of the body and are well aware if a potential death might occur. It should also be told those participating in this holy experience shall also have their own lives changed forever just through their presence with the being who is offered the event of leaving the body for this light experience. Those who are also working from the afterlife are personally chosen by God for this magnificent phenomenon.

As we have stated, every soul who has reached an understanding of this beautiful pure light washing over and throughout the physical body will have this experience in a reincarnation. Should it be chosen for the betterment of the masses then a soul can choose this path again to partake in elevating the energy of others who are ready to follow a path of enlightenment to love and assist the world in reaching a higher level of pure energy.

Many are receiving this magnificent light and love from God to share with your world; it can reach the masses in a very short amount of time. This can change the life of a child even if the wonderment of love is not explained, as it shall remain with the child until reaching an age when they can fully understand the event. Many have come back from this experience and have been gifted with becoming musicians, scientists, or men and women of God to teach and share the event with the masses. It is to be understood that anyone who obtains elevated abilities are gifted and may choose to follow the path of love and wonderment, returning to this Earth as a teacher of goodness. There will be a personal need to have love for all and understand there is life after death. Such a life change for the soul to experience at the cellular level lasts forever, never to return to an unknowing state of mind. There can be peace in the heart for this connection to God and His kingdom.

Some of the scientists of your time shall continue to participate with the medical profession which has yet to understand this gift of light. Others who are working in the medical profession have a glimpse of what is to come and are choosing to work outside of it to dedicate their work to a higher understanding of these times. These souls are residing in a perfect time to experience this magnificent discovery for humans currently living on Earth, as it offers an opportunity to show all beings that you have great potential to see and know your God as one with you at all times. There are old souls who have made the decision to come back to your Earth to bring this understanding to the masses, known as Soldiers of Kindness. They have spent many lifetimes bringing your world and others to a level of love and understanding, offering their knowledge without any monetary desires, for the understanding that there is another way of life waiting each one who is currently calling this Earth home.

Some humans are gifted with the ability to experience life after death and come back to your world to share it; this is a wonderful treasure God has chosen for these souls. Understand they have been gifted with this experience to share with the world but especially for themself. They can see what is ahead and how they may need to make changes moving forward in their life at that time. It is a magnificent gift for any human and one shall be grateful for being the chosen one. Do not take this gift lightly, as when it is you then you have the ability to help others make changes in their lives and correct any fears they may have of their time of season. Anyone who has this experience to share shall see it as one of the blessings in their lifetime.

There are the experiences of psychics and channelers who are gifted to speak of this beautiful energy and shall open to the naysayers a chance to receive this powerful awareness. This shall continue to grow for all within your world and it should be understood that other worlds have experienced vast advancement beyond your Earth and they shall assist you some day to see that man is not alone in their endeavors for advancement. In their lifetime, glimpses shall be offered to each and every human who has a desire to open their mind and heart to your wonderful God who is ever present in the soul. His gift is ready for each of you to participate in this powerful, pure love that is available for all mankind just for the desire to live in beauty, honor and appreciation for your existence and to offer to help all of the ones who are trying to find their way along this path.

Time is never too fast or too slow to see this beauty and feel it move from your heart to your hands, as it is of the moment for each to willingly participate through pure love and understanding. It is God's gift to you to illuminate your world and how powerful you are in God's love!

Hearing Messages

Wow, how many times have we had the thought "It just can't be!" I know that's been my own mind, thinking I had to let something go, believing I couldn't make it come true. Betty, my client in this story, was living exactly like that, keeping truth from herself in every way possible and preventing herself from making a better life.

The call came in on a very busy day, but I felt she needed my help right then, so I dropped what I was doing and provided her a psychic reading on the spot. I realized I had a seeker on my hands that day, but even though Betty heard guiding voices she was not a listener – at least she wasn't until she called me. She had suffered the loss of her first born child at the age of only two months and the baby's father walked away. Since they were not married, there was no baggage when he left. The only baggage was in Betty's heart; the loss of two great loves had reduced her power to a space of deafening silence in her life.

She had been employed in the medical field for 15 years as a nurse and also inherited a good chunk of money, which gave her the strength to carry on when she suffered the loss of her family. She had traveled some, spending the past two years alone. But now finances were beginning to run low and she needed to find work again. The voices in her head had become never-ending; it was time for her to be present to them and try to figure out where life was going to take her.

I saw a big move for Betty and that she was going to change from nursing to a more educational career. When I spoke those words, she quickly shot down being a school teacher, as she did not want the memories of a lost child to haunt her. I suggested she correct that thought so as not to create a block to moving forward, and clarified that it would not be a teacher of children.

I did ask her to spend a few minutes every night for a week looking at a map of the U.S. that she could place on the wall and scan. If Betty hesitated for a moment or two on a particular location, she was to mark it with a pin, making sure it was a pin and not a pen, because a mark seemed too permanent and she would not be able to clean it off.

When she called me for another session, I asked if she had connected with any particular place on this map. Much to my surprise, she had chosen 12 places so I asked how she had chosen them. She said it wasn't any special process, just that she told herself to pin it. An "aha" moment just fell in her lap and it wasn't her own voice! It was Spirit nudging her along, helping her understand, trust and accept her angelic helpers. They had been with Betty all the time; she just wasn't quieting her head to hear them with an open heart. This new-found way of finding her path and trusting divine intervention was so freeing that she left with a new plan to discover her future, knowing she was not alone and never would be again.

Betty is now living in Atlanta, studying to be a nutritionist and working for a teaching hospital as an intern in their nutrition program. When I asked why she chose that field and why Atlanta, she left me with perfect words: "I listened to Spirit and allowed my faith to take me where I needed to go." She is also dating a doctor from another hospital and it sounds like he is a keeper.

No doubt should enter any of our hearts when we get a voice that won't go away. Open the door and invite it into your head via your heart.

* * * * *

It is not what you know; instead it is wanting to know. This will lead you to new things that are in sync with your growth. This is guided information from the ones sent to help you along your path. Understand they are not diminishing your free will; as we have stated before, you are in full control.

You receive many messages from the heavens that can be used for guidance to assist you in finding your way in this life time. These messages come in many ways, as paper would never be able to hold all the information we have for you. As you begin to pay attention to something you hear or feel more than once, understand it can be a repetitive message for you to connect with a spiritual helper chosen for you at this time in your life.

There will be many spiritual helpers as you begin to develop the different levels of life lessons you are here to learn. Many messages go by unnoticed and at such a time Spirit will use another means for you to understand and feel its presence. This usually happens when you are doing something that brings you to a moment of mindful presence.

Since you live in a world of electronic images and voice interaction tools, these have become ways for man to receive common messages from the universe. A telephone ringing, doorbell chiming, a TV program that appears to have a message spoken directly to you can be used as a vehicle from an angelic helper. A newspaper, magazine or something as simple as a license tag has a way of reminding you of a task you need to take on. Some of these messages come to you multiple times for very good reasons, assisting you to notice the patterns that are being sent to you. It's very natural for humans to ask for help and not realize it is right before their eyes. Because of their stress and frustration we know that repetition is needed to awaken the intuitive senses that allow messages to come alive.

The timing of today shall be for the ones who are having issues with decisions of life that come at many turning points and become like a maze for many. Wrong turns are opportunities to break down barriers and turn corners with joy. There are going to be decisions that are made with no hesitation; when you hesitate you cannot embrace gratitude of knowledge that you trust at that time. We sit here and can only watch this process. It is time for all to stop at the corners and follow instinct with faith of help from the universe. There are so many decisions that are wasted on hesitation. Looking back we see the solutions in knowledge. Any action or decision you consider a mistake is really a pearl found in a dark space, just waiting for you to polish and remember what you knew was truth. That is much of what tonight is all about, knowing that knowledge is a gift to walk toward at this time.

In the moment of your mindful breakthrough of our presence to help, you will find that messages are everywhere. Remember, we shall not leave you behind and as the awakening begins to these powerful gifts, you will be nudged to test the messages you receive. This is a day of remarkable blessings and it shall take some time to put trust in such a simple connection, as you will come to know.

This new remarkable tool of awareness shall become a major part of your life if you desire. Look around every day and expect the messages to flow in daily, assisting you in wellness, direction and peace. You will, at some point of time in your life, experience the remarkable gift of divine intervention, a path for you to begin a new direction. This is change that comes quickly and you will not walk this path alone as there will be many angelic helpers supporting you. It is an opportunity for you to find growth and movement in your present life and time. Souls find other careers that can be unlike any desires or training they have experienced. This is a time when many choose a life of service to carry them through their final working years.

Try to understand the present moment you can experience right this instant if you will stop, listen, and trust the love that is there. It is a glorious time to know the universe is showing you the perfection that you manifest when you listen. You are here to make a difference for yourself and others; don't let yourself down; stand tall in pure form. In this way, you will reach heaven's work much more quickly.

GOD'S SOLDIERS

There will come a time, and it is not so far distant, that this life we are speaking about will come, not as devastation that some fear, but when man gains awareness of his responsibility to care for everything that is around him. Spirit works in all things growing here; Earth is a precious place for every entity that God has created. Be it understood, God's Soldiers – Soldier of Patience, Soldier of Peace, Soldier of Kindness, Soldier of Compassion, Soldier of Love, and Soldier of Grace – are custodians of the challenges at hand today, operating with the pureness of mindful love for each man and creature on Earth.

Right now your Earth is operating on a very low frequency and much is hidden from you. The vibration you are in at this time is at a dangerous level for what is yet to be done in the next season of your Earth. God seeks to change the current decay through the work of his Soldiers, very old souls who have made many trips to your world and other worlds. They have mastered the timing of your transitions and how to set up the growth of your awareness. All of them are woven into each soul through God's light; you are a vehicle of great wealth to

your world when you participate in it with their virtues. Think of what you could experience by doing good deeds every moment for one full day. It would create a world beyond your imagination.

God's Soldiers

I am so humbled to be part of this beautiful body of work. When this book was just a dream, I could not begin to understand the power it would bring for each and every one of you holding it in your hands. It is my wish for each of you to join me and act on the words Peter and his non-physical friends are sharing with everyone wanting to make a difference in this world today. We do have the ability, if we choose, to make a difference in others' lives through single acts of kindness, and we will be the receiver of God's beautiful light for this mindful gift of simply sharing goodness.

* * * * *

It shall be the time for every human to comprehend his duties on Earth for living the essence of man. The workings of the Earth as they are known now are not only by the way of life you have chosen to live out; there are many jobs that you could take up as a Soldier of Grace, many a gesture that you could adopt and be in accord with God's Soldiers. It does not have to be a large sum of money or a feast. It can be a mere compliment or gesture to assist in passing higher energy levels from one to another and promoting calmness. As you are aware, it does not give you a high unless you give without any expectation.

This shall not be triggered by the current soul's conscious feeling; rather, it shall just be the intuitive rise of goodness you are gracing your own soul with at this time. There are cells within the body that are activated as they travel to the brain to assist in the emotional high that is felt at the moment of this sharing with another. This is part of the original plan for man – to observe what is being conducted around him at the present time. It shall create a desire for you to assist other humans or creatures who are also living on Earth.

This world is very different from your sister worlds. It is set up to render goodness to every breathing entity surviving here at this time. It is everyone's responsibility to assist with helping hands during crisis or difficulty, and to celebrate with nice words when another light energy being is born. This is what man can do for your world – take responsibility to give love all day without any hesitation and this good energy would wrap your world many times in one day. It would burn off the negative energy affecting all and would give man pause for any decisions to consider a handsome return for themselves first.

Think of what you could experience by doing good deeds every moment for one full day. It would create a world beyond your imagination. You would see new plants, trees, and flowers sprouting in massive elegance and new creatures appearing in wonderment and grandeur to inhabit your Earth for the first time. It would create a heaven of such beauty that all would hold in awe. There would be no need for the existence of corporate media, wars, poverty programs, and borders. Every man, woman and child would be able to move about with love and full responsibility to share what they gain in their life. It would level the world to equal lifestyles and awaken good health, adding many years to every entity's life. The world would appear in a powerful brilliance that no man has seen before.

There will come a time, and it is not so far distant, that this life we are speaking about will come, not as devastation that some fear, but when man gains awareness of his responsibility. And this is definitely part of every human contract coming onto your Earth today. Those who have chosen to remain with their current contract shall begin the cycle of understanding the need to give in all ways known to man today. Much more will become apparent that can be done to accelerate your Earth's vibration and it shall be freely spoken about very soon.

Right now your Earth is operating on a very low frequency and much is hidden from you. This is because the energies are operating on a very dense level and have no way to cleanse, making them dirty, negative, and unable keep up with your soul's circle of light. The vibration you are in at this time is at a dangerous level for what is yet to be done in the next season of your Earth. When we talk about seasons, we are not talking about spring, summer, fall and winter. We are talking about the seasons of souls removing themselves to allow new souls who are better prepared with a fuller view of what is transpiring on your Earth presently. The seasons are decades of decay, which God seeks to change through the work of his Soldiers, whom we speak about many times in these writings. They have always been here for you; you just have not been aware of their existence. They shall bring betterment of your future and your world.

Understand, these Soldiers are very old souls who have made many trips to your world and other worlds. They have mastered the timing of your transitions and how to set up the growth of your awareness. These Soldiers are working in pods all over the world in every country known to man. They can be considered the highest of helpers for only one leader of the highest and that is God. He is the gracious, loving Caretaker of every man, woman and child. God is your giver of light and love, shared equally by each soul upon this Earth. God's light shines much brighter through his Soldiers who are here working for the good of all worlds.

Be aware they are many; they are effective in their duties; and they never leave anyone behind – they represent Grace, Love, Peace, Compassion, Kindness and Patience, all woven into each soul through God's light. The Soldier of Patience is one of the highest in the land for you, as these very old soul Soldiers deal with all of the virtues that the other Soldiers must master to acquire their success in getting world awareness to where it is needed at this time. So be it understood, God's Soldiers are custodians of the challenges at hand today, operating with the pureness of mindful love for each one on Earth.

Soldier of Patience

I see the work of the Soldiers as so benevolent and I know you will feel the same as you read this lovely work of two beautiful Soldiers of Patience. It is so comforting to know that God's presence is in all of our lives to help us complete our own tasks at hand. The reading I am about to share with you comes from an older couple, Lois and Paul, who worked overseas for a Christian charity during their 30-plus years of marriage, helping rebuild homes in horrendously war-torn and weather-beaten areas of the world.

They had three daughters over those years, each born in a different country, and lived the same as those they were there to serve. The last child, Lily, was born with a cleft palate and deformities of her mouth. Not one time did they make the decision to leave their beloved work due to her issues, but chose to use the doctors who visited these countries on a regular basis and also volunteered their time and skills to assist those in dire need for a chance at a better life in these poor areas of the world. The family was so dedicated to help the under-privileged that they put themselves on a waiting list for Lily's surgery so that others in more urgent circumstances could be seen first in the short time of the doctors' visits.

The psychic reading for this couple was a birthday gift from Lily who had settled in the states and was expecting her third child. When she called to make their appointment, we had a chance to talk about her own health. She spoke of the cherished childhood she and her sisters experienced over the years and felt she had never missed out on anything. She said in many ways her disabilities seemed normal to her as she had played with many children who were far worse off than she was. We talked about Lois and Paul's adventures over the years and how it was getting time for them to make some decisions about retirement, so they were excited to speak with me.

I sat in stillness for a while before the reading, as I felt the loving energy of Lois and Paul, knowing it would be a wonderful experience for me and realizing they were a very special couple. When the call came in, I was taken aback by their soft-spoken voices, and wondered if they could sense what a calming influence they must be within whatever community they were currently serving. Earlier I had seen a small group of women waiting in a medical clinic, some with babies and toddlers, realizing their deep ability to serve with loving hearts. They talked about the families they anticipated they would miss as they were ready to make the transition to living in full retirement. They had spent their lives putting their needs on hold to be able to offer a better way for so many by helping them achieve skills to support their families.

I saw Lois and Paul moving back to be near their daughters and the several grandchildren they had not seen for a while. I told them I saw a large farm area that was close by and asked if they had thought about their living arrangements. It really did feel like they would need some land to spread out on; they certainly would not be city dwellers. They actually got excited about the possibility of having some wide open space that the kids could visit.

But the main thing I kept seeing and feeling was that their volunteering days were not over. When I told them of this vision, they both laughed, as they felt the same thing, even though the girls just wanted mom and dad home and staying in one house for a long time, catching up on holidays and getting to know those grandchildren that were still to come, as two daughters were expecting. We spoke of some more fun things coming down the pipeline for them and a final promise of another reading when they got settled.

I received a letter from Lois and Paul about year later and sure enough, they were living on a farm not far from their daughters and there was more good news than that. They had partnered with one of the Christian charities they had served and decided to open their home to families coming to America with children who had severe disabilities, offering them a place to live while undergoing the surgeries that could change their lives. Many came for amputations and new limbs would be made for these children, all of which take ample time. They were giving these families the opportunity to stay together as a family while they received this much-needed care.

Their own girls were involved in this new venture and the older grandchildren were learning the ropes of selfless offering even in their early stages of life. The daughters laughed at the big dinners they remembered as kids, playing with all of the animals that were how the local families had paid them, and certainly not on the table for food! Lisa regaled that she was the one who wanted to have horses for the kids, which had not come to the farm yet, but she had a feeling they were getting close to showing up, as the house became filled with youngsters.

They worked daily in helping the visiting families and their children learn to cope with the remarkable changes that were coming so quickly in their lives and to handle the sad cases when the outcome was not so positive. There is no doubt, these lovely people were definitely Soldiers of Patience for so many and even in retirement their calling was still to calm, care, and comfort those needing a little more time to get to the next level in life with the gifts that patience gives of peace, love, kindness, grace, and compassion.

* * * * *

Patience is a gift of the mind and does not always operate within humans for the goodness of their lives in these times. Much can be said of the need to work on this great emotion that can slow the mind to give it a chance to fire the electrical current in the brain and enlarge the space of gray matter to increase its optimum working order. Patience is any motion of self-control that allows the body and the mind to awaken the cells to connect in proper sequence.

If the emotion of anger or any negative energy shall appear due to a misfire of electrical current, it will rob the heart of the ability to hold a very consistent rhythm and to send the circulation through the body that keeps all functions operating at their best. Such an unfavorable period of blood flow can cause a detour and break vessels due to the overheating of the blood cells, starting a malfunction that can bring about death or a blockage for the brain. Should this trauma occur, it shall cause the brain cells to tighten and enlarge from stress, then die off. This can be prevented by using one's breath to slow the heart and help the circulation function to not generate so many barriers if the body becomes heated, which explode the cells that are not driving the correct level of blood flow to an area.

With a small turn of mindset and the love that is created through patience and calmness, brain cells may be restored as additional ones can be grown. Understand that any external energy can be negative and look to continue its existence by attaching to healthy cell tissue.

Calm your heart and allow your hand to hold another's in a time of need, to take one's hand and help this soul up and walk steadily as it removes itself from fear and anger. Remember, the touch of another human with love from heart to hand can create a new path for the cells to begin lightening the load on the organs of the body. Welcome all that comes from love and understanding, that you all will find a path which many have walked before, even as you leave new footsteps imprinted in the sand. It shall not be so hard to slow the body's function to a kinder, more thoughtful way of feeling and thinking, sharing one's hand as this shall always prove to be a blessing more for the giver than the receiver. Should you be the receiver, accept this love, understanding, and kindness, knowing that a Soldier of Patience took the time to bring you to your own greater patience by sharing theirs, with their heart and hand.

Understand all Soldiers of Patience come at the proper time and not only offer help to a weathered human whose struggles are affecting their body. They are also there to offer assistance to that soul's loved ones and empower them as well with the loving energy of calmness and benevolence for their healing and a better appreciation for the value of slowing emotions that are out of control during their crisis.

As we have discussed, these revered Soldiers of Patience are the highest level of Soldiers that God sends to your Earth to intervene when necessary and protect the lives of wearied humans who are on an overload of anxiety for whatever the soul's work is calling them to conduct within their contracts at this time. A contract may be a crisis of many souls who are working in tandem, where the negative energy that has attached to their situation can cause unnecessary harm if they lose sight of the real work at hand and suffer an imbalance of their minds to resolve things. Be it understood that Soldiers of Patience will send a call to other Soldiers that are properly needed to complete this work without the need to displace a soul at this time. All of God's Soldiers are fully aware of the best sequence of events and shall give special treatment to any soul currently needing adjustments of the body, so it may stay healthy to finish its work even if that work is not their contract agreement.

It should also be understood, a Soldier of Patience shall make a call for all Soldiers to work throughout your world in times of war and unrest; such a call is sent in the blink of an eye to make adjustments when needed and so as not to disturb the contracts that are being played out at the time. It is not for these Soldiers to stop any planned contract crisis in the world that is created by harm or deviance on the part of your world's evil entities working presently at levels unknown to mankind. This shall be shown to all in due time to come for the exercise of human understanding when God shall offer this information by whatever method shall be chosen.

It shall be seen for each soul operating in whatever age and stage of life that the work of the Soldiers of these namesakes shall offer Peace, Love, Kindness, Compassion, Grace and Patience, touching each and every soul within their many human life times. As we have said before, God's Soldiers are in great numbers, working both as physical and non-physical, and are operating within every age group on Earth at this time. Some are recognized by the gifted while most work quietly and unnoticed, attaching pure love to each drop of rain that shall fall and every breath taken by man and creature alike. It shall be a grand day when the work of these Soldiers is acknowledged in a world that understands the need for this beautiful energy to be a constant flow for all who are here in whatever life they have chosen, when the Earth is awash with the purest love of God's presence.

Soldier of Peace

While each of God's soldiers stand out and meticulously convey God's work at his highest and most trusted level, Soldiers of Peace have come up in several of my readings and this one today provides another opportunity to experience their magnificent loving task at hand.

This is a special story about Pat, an older woman I have done readings for a few times over the years. Those calls always related to her military career when she was facing a deployment into a war zone hospital, as she had been a nurse before her enlistment. This particular call started with catching up on her life for the past two years, including her forthcoming retirement from the military. Pat's main questions for me this day concerned her desire to leave nursing but stay in the role of helping the families of lost soldiers in some way.

I asked about a framed family tree I was seeing over her piano and she laughed, as she knew I had a knack for seeing some strange things in my readings. I felt such a connection to this piece and I knew she had a future with an unusual twist. When I asked who had helped her with the work on her family tree, she told me about an investigator, Tom, who did it for fun and that she was thinking about calling him for some help getting started with her new genealogy hobby. Pat had never married and was intrigued with that kind of research; she felt a strong pull to helping people find out about their past. She had seen many soldiers lose their lives and there had been times when some of their belongings would be delayed in getting shipped out with the body and would get lost in transit. She talked about how she felt so badly for these families and had made a promise that if her life played out like she wanted, then she would help those in need close that gap.

No question, Pat had a new career coming up in a very short time, but she still had a few more decisions to make in the next month, as I saw a major move to another country. When I asked about the move, she got a little unsure that making a move might mean she was making this career change too soon.

It was time to stop the reading because I wanted her to make the connection with others about her possible new adventure, so we made an appointment in three weeks. Her next call came through with a sense of uneasiness about the business, as she had made a few calls and her old friends had moved on from their genealogy work. I could tell Pat was having second thoughts about her career decision to leaving nursing and was back to square one.

Although the business was somewhat off track, she did get a call about a position for a part-time nursing position in Hawaii that could become full-time and the beach was where she wanted to be, so she had made a reservation for the trip and was scheduled to interview the next day. That was really her happy moment but I knew it was to be short-lived when I saw a big Red Cross symbol on a truck. So I mentioned that and it turned out she had been thinking about doing some volunteer work for them if she moved to Hawaii.

She called the next week to let me know she had gotten the position and was prepared to move by the end of the week. She said I was right about the Red Cross lead, as they had called her and she was due to start in a few weeks, on call for disasters that fit into her timetable with work. I *decided to hold off with any further calls for a while, as I knew I would be hearing from her in a month or so.*

Time can really fly by and that it did with Pat. When I heard from her again, she was just about to take her military retirement. She was so excited; she had taken some time to enjoy the beaches, was hiking, and now had life that she treasured. She had started a genealogy business and was able to use it while working for the Red Cross in Indonesia. She had found identifying information with some personal papers which were unclaimed, and was able to trace down the family and return them. She got bit by the bug and was taking trips around the world doing exactly what I had seen for her and was loving it.

As she moved into her dream, Pat was able to connect with a group of hobbyists, giving her the opportunity to teach the search processes to others for tracing family lineage, and was working on some family cases where soldier husbands had been lost many wars ago. She also got a real bonus in the endeavors for her new life, which was the real walking, talking investigator she had known many years ago. Doing similar work all over the world, Tom had put a ring on her finger and the name of his business changed to reflect the new union of experience and marriage.

The more she spoke of her work, the more I was sure Pat was in the company of one of the most respected of God's helpers, a Soldier of Peace. I am convinced she is in training for this benevolent being and will be bringing closure to military families and peace for the loved ones left behind for many years to come. It sure does prove that when you are making plans, setting goals, and working the vision, it pays to have a strong faith that God never closes one door without opening another with grace.

* * * * *

The Soldiers of Peace work in all corners of your universe and honor all beings throughout God's worlds with the same desire to hold each in the highest level of love and kindness. It is of great beauty when you are in the presence of these mighty Soldiers as their stature is as large or as small as needed. To be in their company is to be a humbled caring soul who has chosen to live in complete calmness and benevolence. To keep the peace of God's worlds, these beautiful beings have the ability to touch each heart and melt the mind to advance to a higher level of love, helping correct the ego of all breathing entities, and realize a desire for peace within the heart.

It is not to be said that Earth's beings are peaceful at all times. It shall be understood that in some seasons of your worlds you have karmic debt to correct, while other times you have completed your debt in other lives, so you will have contracts to assist with those who have chosen to find peace and assist your worlds with loving consciousness. This opportunity shall offer a correction for all to grow into an understanding of the need to stop the destruction of God's children. The Soldiers of Peace shall help you stand up to find goodwill and allow the Earth to change its energy, correcting itself to offer a home for all beings and allow every species a show of growth once again.

Through this, much can be said for the Soldiers of Peace, as they are not just the gatekeepers to stop self-destruction of your world today through wars; they are also the peacemakers of understanding the need for love and communion with others over a lifetime. All wars of past and future shall carry a burden for man to collect karma and reincarnate for payment of unforgiven deeds created by man's misguided actions. These Soldiers of Peace walk the past seasons of battlefields to help souls find their way home to rest and comfort, and shall do so for any future seasons of battlefields created by man's egos and harmful actions of control by those in power. Their tasks in these endeavors shall go on as long as your worlds are in existence and they shall honor all human soldiers without judgment for their actions in these wars and conflicts, no matter the karma created.

They shall call on the other groups of God's Soldiers and shall be tasked to participate when needed for the lost ones of war and those families left behind without correct closure and comfort. It shall not be unusual for the many classes of God's Soldiers to work together in small groups to assist a community for the adjustment of love and understanding, as well as of peace to work in harmony and prosperity for the betterment of man. Be it understood that God does not leave loved ones behind to grieve and feel the pain for many seasons to come. This is why all of God's Soldiers were created, to offer their heart to hand in assistance for all mankind to find peace and know their loved ones are bound by the love of your God.

The Soldiers of Peace will always be the gatekeepers for wars and will always play a part in all factors of man's existence to right the seasons as they continue to evolve. Their work is to assist each human and creature to stop and view the world from a different perspective and allow them to see their part in making this world a beautiful paradise for all here today as well as tomorrow's new souls. It can be said this work can help assist in awakening to a spiritual path, the growth of kindness, and the desire to love and help each other find the way to prosper in this lifetime. Honor and know that a Soldier of Peace does not need armor or control to create a state of calmness for all humans, just a powerful devotion to grant love and offer peace for the betterment of your world.

Anger is another emotion these wonderful beings assist in correcting for each soul and the environment. Be it understood that a world of anger can be a collection of many layers that need to be taken away. These Soldiers offer man help to accomplish their good deeds by permeating the environment with love to temper this negativity that creates a space of decay. Correcting the effects of anger is a daily job for all who call this Earth home.

Anger and negativity can destroy a community of not only man but its structures, as they also have energy-based lives. Every structure and the Earth it is built on has a heart and mindful existence, feels the harm from man's hand, and shall show this in the very material it is made of, as it begins to corrode. Without love, all things of your Earth shall starve and decay, losing the energy God has granted for man's protection and comfort, gifted to all entities of all worlds. To thrive in any world, God has given the help of these Soldiers of Peace to assist and find harmony, comfort, and happiness.

It shall be of free will for all man and creatures to decide and understand the value of loving others and placing their hand in another's for offering the pure loving state of peace. No man shall survive in this world with all of God's gifts without the comfort of another human or creature, nor shall it be God's desire for that season to come to pass. Ponder the magnificent wonder of God's land with another being to share this gift with and go in peace to find it.

Soldier of Kindness

Kindness is an emotion that humanity can spread across the world at rapid speed when the mind is operating for the highest good. I have so many readings under my belt regarding how thoughts and actions regarding kindness and grace influence how we live our lives and help others along the way. This reading is about Allison, a young lady who was a superstar according to her mother but lately she seemed to be going through a period of anxiety and just wanted to sleep all of the time. So her mother felt a reading with me might be able to get her out of her funk.

When the call came through, my first impression of Allison's difficulty was her negative attitude and when I asked about it, she was defensive and almost argumentative. I could see this reading was going to be uphill for a while, but I knew there was a sincere heart hurting that wanted to come out of that guarded shell.

I asked about her years as a Girl Scout selling cookies and always winning her troop's patch and she smiled, leaving me the opening I needed to make a believer out of her. We talked about her shelves of trophies for sports, dancing, and childhood beauty pageants. Allison began to open up about having accomplishments but never feeling part of the winning crowd. No matter how many victories she was able to share with her teammates, she was always alone and really did not understand why. She was a good teammate yet felt left out even as she moved on in her life, past school and into the work world. I asked if she had ever worked with positive affirmations and her reaction was to laugh and say it was such a waste of her time; she just wanted friends and not to become the latest new age guru.

I could see the current core of her negativity was anxiety about her job. Allison certainly was ready for something new because she was working for a couple who owned a small elderly home and kept her in constant fear of being let go. They were always threatening to close and not be weighed down with poor government funding and having a hard time meeting payroll. I brought up the idea of a career change for her and told her I kept seeing hockey players all around her. She mentioned a job that was being advertised at the local hockey facility for a position she had thought of checking out. She was surprised I brought this up, as she had only just seen an ad for it in a window as she was dropping off her brother for his hockey practice the day before. I knew the job at the hockey rink was perfect for her and felt certain she would get the position.

Yet she still needed to deal with her negativity and when I brought it up to Allison, she seemed relieved to finally see how hard her attitude was on herself and her friends. They had never really left her, so much as she had driven them away. No matter how much she accomplished, she was just angry and negative; no one wanted to be around her.

Back to the affirmations, we explored once again how important they were for her to say them out loud every day to begin creating change and prophesying a happy and content future. I had her write down 10 affirmations starting with being worthy of a group of close friends, a job that would be steady, and anything else she wanted to accomplish in the next year. She was to call back in a month and we would see how far she had moved forward in creating a life of happiness, grace, accepting kindness from others and above all, giving kindness to others and feeling the effects of this powerful energy.

Needless to say, Allison called with news of her new position at the local hockey arena helping the kids with skating lessons and setting up events for the children. She was also taking coaching lessons from one of the instructors and wanted to teach kids how to show kindness and consideration through being team players and treating others in their sports competitions with respect.

I am so happy to report that she has moved on to becoming certified as a coach and is now teaching classes on positive approaches to achieving a life of kindness and personal success. Her affirmations are now a daily ritual;

she has even created her own affirmations and uses them with the kids at the arena – and they are loving it. She also noticed she was feeling so much better physically that she didn't need the naps anymore and was losing some weight with all of her newfound energy.

She said I had taught her to be happy with what she has accomplished for herself and to use this happiness to offer at least one person a word of kindness daily. And the compliments Allison gets in return are giving her the courage to go for her dreams every day, one by one.

* * * * *

The soul enters into a child's body at birth with a pristine level of openness, a state of being called the grace of kindness that begins in the birth canal. The first encounters of touch from human contact will stay with the child and imprint the soul from that very moment. The child is no longer a closed vessel waiting for life to begin; in the moment of the first breath its impressions are part of the soul's contract which is not remembered at this time. Each moment shall be experienced just as the soul agreed upon to fulfill the duties of a Soldier of Kindness.

Be it understood the child who is to be a Soldier of Kindness begins its spiritual growth at this time, develops its personality, and uses its free will more readily to create its permanent character stamp and begin its work. The child can experience an alteration for the beginning of its work path at the time it is born; contract changes shall be known by each newborn's spiritual handlers who accept changes that better the work to be done for that lifetime. These changes are thought out and addressed before the contract is complete, and should the handlers perceive the work of this soul as one of God's Soldiers of Kindness needed for a later date, the soul group is prepared to alter the contract as needed. Plans are changed by allowing the group a better understanding of their spiritual work to be done, regardless of man's Earthly timetable.

It should also be known the soul groups that these Soldiers of Kindness are working in represent other Soldiers also awaiting assignments for their work to begin. Soldiers are sent in the blink of an eye to whatever challenges require them in the changing conditions of your world. This can be seen happening at rapid speed no matter what transpires, to help all souls calling Earth home. God has his Soldiers working in all areas of the world and at times; some more evolved beings are sent to assist when needed from the sister worlds that are working peacefully in your universe at this time. We have discussed their assistance previously in this book and there shall not be fear attached to their presence in your world. This emotion of fear has been produced by lack of knowledge and it shall change for all in the near future of light years. One of the roles of God's Soldiers is to prepare humans for the coming time to actively be using all of the emotions the Soldiers are assisting you with at this time.

The loving parents of this child are also working as God's Soldiers of Kindness and are not the only humans that God will choose to participate in the child's contract. This shall begin at the moment of the first touch at birth from the doctor and birthing attendants; these humans are all special souls operating also as Soldiers of Kindness. They shall embrace their job of passing the pure love of God's creation and emitting the highest level of energy for this young being to begin its path on Earth, regardless of the age at which its work shall actually begin. There is special consideration for this young soul to experience a pure loving energy and be guarded from any trauma by the love of these beings.

If the work of a Soldier of Kindness commences in the early years of his or her life, the opportunities abound for this young being to assist others in their need of the emotion called kindness. This child shall work among all ages, nationalities, races, and genders, showing remarkable ability to comprehend the need for action through the smallest gesture of bestowing a smile or being held by a stranger who seeks the love that only a child can bring at that time. Older children are chosen to help younger ones experience love they have not known until they are befriended, and they bond from the hunger for kindness and mercy.

A Soldier of Kindness is born into a full life of giving, always knowing when kindness is needed and offering this emotion without any desire for return favor. It should also be noted a Soldier of Kindness child shall always stand out among the pods of young souls and will grow into an adult of pure love in presence no matter the circumstances that the soul shall be experiencing.

Soldiers of Kindness shall teach this emotion to others so they will feel love and share it with other humans and creatures they meet along the way as they continue their life path. At such a time, the physical body shall be adjusted to its highest level of operation, based on a state of being that occurs when kindness and compassion are presented to souls in need of this energy. This adjustment is to assist the soul in making the right choices of goodness and grace and having a complete understanding of its need to return this energy to your world. The only desire of such a one is a feeling of contentment from giving kindness and helping others in their life experiences. There shall be more of these loving Soldiers to assist all creatures and man to live and spread this energy throughout your world, offering unconditional love for mankind at this time.

The purpose of God's Soldiers has been spoken about many times in these writings and it is the will of many non-physical beings to assist you to gain awareness of these old souls always willing to offer you kindness and to show by example the rewards you shall reap by following in their footsteps. Be it understood, the Soldiers of Kindness are assisting mankind as early as birth and shall continue until they are called home to God's kingdom. There is purpose in every moment of life and it is the job of the Soldiers to help each human acquire the understanding of love and the desire to offer kindness from heart to hand.

Soldier of Compassion

I am not sure I have addressed the process of clients who are referred to me, but I request no information regarding the person I am going to read for. It is so important to keep the contact with the new client clear of any bits and pieces that their friend may know about them; that way, the session is free of any information that could distract the purity of its message.

This reading came to me on Christmas Eve a few years ago, a referral from a special client who is always helping others along the way. She seems to find them just at the right time and, of course, she never misses a beat. This one has a special place in my heart, too. Well, not to get too sappy, here we go!

When Leslie's call came in, I could feel this young lady's immediate desire to get to work on her issues; it was almost too quick a start for someone wanting help from a psychic. She had every question laid out in order, like a Type A personality, so I knew Leslie was not fitting her square-peg self into that round-hole called her life.

I asked when her parents had passed and if they were both doctors. She was a little taken back that I had picked up so quickly on her family past. I also saw that she had been working in the medical field as well, but at a lower level than the picture I was receiving of her education.

She started talking about her mom, a nurse case manager for a large hospital, and her dad, a neurologist in private practice. During a trip home from a combination family reunion and Christmas holiday, they were killed in a car accident. The wounds were still fresh and it had stopped Leslie in her tracks for any thoughts of life direction. As she was the only child, she quit her job to make the arrangements when it happened and went home to take care of the family estate. She talked about her parents being such compassionate medical servants all of her life, and opened up about the lack of emotions in her family.

At that very moment, I saw an older version of a nurse's hat and a big box of Band Aids that was on a shelf really high, with Leslie sitting on the floor crying over her bleeding knee. Then the view went to her first communion and she was standing on the steps of the vestibule, looking out to see her mom Brenda and her nanny, but her dad, Eric, was missing. When I brought this up, the floodgate of tears began to flow. She talked about her parents being so dedicated to everyone else that she had felt she was not important enough to be loved like they loved all of the sick people they were taking care of. She had grown into a hardened soul that felt compassion was a waste of time, not meant for everybody – just those who got sick.

Here's where the sappy side of me comes in. I felt so saddened that Leslie lacked the ability to feel someone's compassion from growing up without knowing unconditional love and for the pain she was going through. We talked for a while longer and I asked whether she had ever written a diary or if she'd found her mom or dad had any diaries when she cleaned out the house. She thought about the books that she had found from her dad's library, but had not read them or even opened one; that was too far down her list of things to do.

I asked her to take a look at Eric's diaries, especially the years since her birth, to see if Brenda had left anything behind in a box of pictures or mementoes, and to create a list of her own writings. We would talk again in two weeks and make a solid plan to get her live back on target. I just had a really deep feeling this young lady's parents loved her very much and Allison had somehow lost sight of it from so much time in private boarding schools and not having the kind of bond she had wanted with them.

When the call came in Allison seemed somewhat more at ease with the reading, almost like a research student. She was excited to talk about letters her dad had written to her mom while he was traveling overseas teaching in prestigious medical schools. He had been writing special notes all along about how proud he was of her and somehow she had missed getting them from her mother when she was home for school breaks.

She was now beginning to feel the love and compassion her parents had felt for her as she began to piece together the many writings about how much she was appreciated and how proud they were of her. Deep into Brenda's packet of letters, Allison had found an envelope written to her that she had never seen before and when she opened it a locket fell out with her initials on it. She was shocked to realize her dad had written her such a long letter about missing her, being so proud of her, and feeling sorry to have spent so much time away from her. The locket was to be a gift for her communion that Brenda had overlooked giving her.

I asked if she had given any thought to the future and the answer was a real surprise. She had finished school with a teaching degree but only worked a short time in a nursing home because she was drawn to older adults, and now decided to go back to school and acquire a business degree which would only take her 18 months. She had the money to buy a small home for the elderly, possibly an Alzheimer's facility. She was so captivated by her dad's work that she had stayed in touch with some of his employees; she could see who might be interested in a new career. When we closed the reading that day, Allison expressed much gratitude for the path she now found herself on, which might never have come to light if we had not talked about her dad's diaries.

Interestingly, she found a box of poems her mom had written, as well as several files of artwork and poems she had written herself while she was away at school that her mother had meticulously compiled. Looking at these made her think about an opportunity to teach poetry for fun. Not only had Allison found her confidence, but she felt the desire to share compassion with anyone who might want to learn to write poetry, or could use some company and just needed a friend to spend time with. She even talked about getting some of that poetry framed for the new Alzheimer's unit she was destined to own and operate.

This young lady had been given a beautiful gift of love from the past and it opened up a bright future straight from her heart to hands.

* * * * *

All of God's Soldiers have important roles for humans and like beings in all of God's worlds; there is no difference in their tasks regardless of where they are working at this time. It should be understood that all Soldiers of God are completely centered in all beings of God's children and will always be working to help center each human or entity to a place of kindness and love for other souls. It is not for each soul to come to into your world with this built into the body as just an emotion; it shall be learned.

Compassion is considered a high regard for another being of whatever species, showing loving energy and radiating a pure heart that shall have no boundaries. Much can be said about a newborn child experiencing the tears of its mother when she is blessed in those first few moments of embracing this beautiful gift of God's love. These tears are the first sign of compassion being imprinted upon the child's DNA, activating a drop of love within the young soul's heart and mind. The tears are pure from the energy that connects these two souls, that of pulsing, bright, illuminating light giving nourishment for the soul to cry out to the world and set this luminous energy on its way to expand to all who come forward and be present for this birth.

It is to be noted that a child shall understand the emotions of sadness and fear, giving their small gestures of new expressions through the holding of one's finger or touching another human ever so lightly. A Soldier of Compassion has carried this child to the birth canal for its Earth entry and shall be given the job of providing for this young soul the opportunity to expand its growth and have a clear understanding to build on this love of no boundaries called compassion.

It is the work of a Soldier of Compassion to introduce to the child feelings of love and tenderness for all species, just as it is the work of any human with this emotion who is among those contracted to participate in teaching this child of God. There is an agreement that is unspoken and known by all Soldiers to participate when needed to expand on other qualities of character for a child or anyone who is not in alignment with this emotion. Love and understanding the need to create bonds with other humans and creatures is one of God's greatest gifts to all who call the worlds of the heavens home.

This job is actually to teach and create a memory that shall remain with each soul and, if for any reason the gesture of compassion of the heart shall wane, it is the work of these great Soldiers to place humans in an environment that fosters the love that emits from their heart to another, to assist in understanding all trials of life each human shall experience.

To know compassion and feel the beauty of sharing this benevolent energy is the decision left to each soul after the initial assistance that they are given at this very young age. All parents are aware this shall be part of the child's growth of the heart, to reach out for the help of mankind and feel attached to this energy. There shall be no being abiding a life on any world that will not be given the opportunity to embrace this gift of holding others in high regard. The expression is of free will but the permanent imprint on the soul's DNA will create its own personal desire to activate the heart to be able to give freely this gift of compassion.

To know you can and will give compassion to another is one of God's greatest gifts for man and it is not to be taken lightly when this beautiful expression comes to light in the heart of another. The Soldiers of Compassion are to share with all humans this need and shall help them understand this work, God's love for others. This is how you are able to piece together a more lasting love of your fellow man in God's creatures. Without the opportunity to share and feel the rewards of caring, the body shall reject all emotions of goodness. Allow the body to generate the fluids that are needed to nourish itself, and know that for every tear that is shared in compassion for another human or creature, you are watering all of God's children here on your Earth. It shall come to each soul within its lifetime even though some are not receivers of the full knowledge of this beautiful task of loving others until later times in life.

This can be seen when an elder is feeling the loneliness of existence and a need to touch a stranger. That is the job of a Soldier of Compassion, to see to it that each human, healthy or frail, is constantly reminded of their need to express love. It can be understood that although the Soldiers are not allowed to change your free will, it shall be their job to help each one feel their heart with this pure light of love on a regular basis when they are called on to assist those in need.

No life, human or creature, shall leave this world without giving and receiving compassion. It is through the process of death that the soul fully understands the role of giving compassion freely, upon the separation of the soul from the body into the arms of loved ones and other Soldiers of God to assist in the final moments of crossing into God's kingdom.

Soldiers of Compassion have graced your worlds since the beginning moments of God's creation you now call home. They are the oldest souls, who will never give up their jobs, not because they are required by God to leave the honor but because they radiate the most pure and luminous love, shine brightly in its beautiful, white light, and embrace with the gift of benevolence each and every soul and species of God's kingdom. Every moment of their beautiful energy they share with all beings, shining their light brighter to pave the way home, acknowledging a magnificent journey well done.

Soldier of Love

Love is so needed to truly touch another human on a deep and meaningful level, and the desire to do this lasts forever if this is an interest for yourself. The psychic reading I am going to talk about here is one of acceptance of love in following your heart for this passion.

The call came at a really busy time, what with readings and writing a book that is yet to be finished, mostly due to the time I spend on my appointments for readings. I felt a very big pull to help this particular young woman, trying her best to get her life on track, what with going to school and helping pay family bills as her dad was ill and her mom was taking care of him full time.

Kim's reading was scheduled for early the next day and I had a tough time getting her off my mind until then. I got a feeling she was sinking into a state of emotional distress. I kept seeing her standing by an elderly woman's side at what appeared to be a hospice center and pushing the woman outside in the garden to sit and play cards with her.

The next morning when Kim called, she was so anxious for the reading, saying she was feeling somewhat worried about whether she could get a job without having finished school. Her father with late-stage Alzheimer's was getting harder for her mom, Julie, to take care of, so Kim was needed at home. Even full time, she had two more years of school to get her degree in nursing and wanted to go on to possibly be a doctor – so many years away!

She was such a light, walking among the sick and elderly. In many ways, this young girl was a healer in training. I told her the vision I'd had of her. She got pretty excited for the chance to work in hospice and spoke of how much she loved to go to the retirement homes and pass time with the elderly, sitting outside and pointing out the butterflies.

Much to Kim's amazement, she remembered she had just spent the day before playing cards with Cliff, an elderly man whose life had been spent as a doctor in the South. He loved to talk about how he had helped so many for free, as they did not have the money nor would he take it from them. Cliff spoke of hardly being able to pay the office rent and personal bills. But God had always been good to him and he made it all the way until he retired when he suffered a stroke. This young lady had the same kind-heartedness this old man had and was prepared to do whatever she could do to be of service to others, walking away every night knowing she'd filled people's hearts with love, the main thing they needed.

The very next week I got a call to tell me she had gotten a position with the local hospice and she would start school online the very next semester. Kim was being assisted by *a Soldier of Love, just starting to find her way, an old soul with the credentials to make her lot in life one of helping others receive the food of love, just like the butterflies she was pointing out every day to her loving patients.*

* * * * *

The time of the day matters for any soul wanting to connect with the wonders of the universe and the light of the heavens, which we know as love. Mornings are so fresh and breathing into a new day brings peace and visions of your energy reacting with both body and mind. The novelty of this vibrant time is the birth of a clean day, when thoughts have not yet awakened as you get out of bed.

Sit in quiet, if only for a few moments, to feel the soles of your feet come alive and allow the energy to spread into each part of your body. As it reaches your arms, place your hands over your heart to usher love into the beginning of your day and realize it is the wonder of life. Intend to give and receive love in every aspect of your day and allow it to touch each soul you come in contact with during your waking moments.

Make a ritual of this feeling and know that the energy of love is one of greatness. Using this feeling every day will trigger a chain reaction for you to go out into the world with the love of a butterfly flying here and there, nurturing all things of beauty and leaving a small piece of this loving energy with everyone. This allows love to permeate each energy field and presents every creature and man with such a gift, to feel and nourish their own needs with this powerful energy.

Imagine if every human woke up in the early morning, willing love from the soles of their feet into their body and touching their heart for it to continue its journey up to the most reverent crown, and then releasing this love into the world for all to partake of it. If all souls did this every day there would be no negative energy to collect and cause such mayhem in this world you call home. Many have no idea as they pass one who has practiced this lovely ritual, why the love they feel in that moment is so immense. It is a contagious energy that is free, costing you nothing more than the time it takes your body to make a mental note and emit this energy. It is power beyond belief! Come into your space and a Soldier of Love shall assist you.

The evening is also a wondrous time to sit in silence, fill your heart with love, and feel the energy flow through your body. A Soldier of Love shall support you in placing your hands on your heart and feeling the love travel up into your crown. Imagine magnificent love streaming from the top of your head, following a path to another soul who needs the presence of additional love and allowing that energy to go to the ones who need it for their body to sleep and heal any negativity they currently may be exposed to.

You are a vehicle of great wealth to your world when you participate in this practice. It is a powerful gift you are giving and you will be blessed with more than you could ever anticipate experiencing in your life. You can change your heart and help others with their needs. Go with the love and peace of the evening. This shall become an automatic ritual for you through the help of a Soldier of Love, as it is with the assistance of this wondrous being that you fill up with the warm, pure light of love all day and every day. Should you find a time when you are forgetful of this ritual, it shall be a time for you to call on a Soldier of Love.

Soldier of Grace

The material here honestly feels like it was wholly written by Peter and the non-physical beings especially for this client – as always, there is a fitting place for each of their writings. April, a referral client, called me one day and wanted to make an appointment for her dad, Glenn, whom she felt was at a crossroads in his life and although he had never experienced a psychic reading before, she felt he would be open to it.

I called Glenn the very next day and when he answered the phone, I could tell he was pretty nervous. I assured him I was harmless and asked him to wait a few minutes before he started talking. I had received a huge block of information about him that I was certain would be exactly the answer to his issues. I saw Glenn sitting on the back of a white truck unloading plants of different colors and stacking beautiful stone blocks beside a big dirt pile. Then the vision shifted to a sign a man was painting on the side of his truck. I knew this was the beginning of a wonderful reading for both of us.

I told him what I saw and asked if by some chance he was currently working for the city. Astonished that I knew this, he explained he had worked for the city over 25 years as a groundskeeper for the parks and was being asked to consider a retirement package, as they were going to outsource the work due to budget changes. He was at a loss for what he could do for a job, because working at a nursery was not enough money for him, but he loved plants so much and being outdoors made him feel so happy.

I asked if he would consider his own nursery business and apply to the city for the contract of the city parks, plantings, and upkeep throughout the city. Definitely, it would give him the work and money he needed. Glenn got very excited and then slowly began to going into the fear mode, as he had no experience of contracts and the value he could ask for the jobs.

This was the time to suggest he call April and ask her for some assistance in getting him the accountant to help plan this all out and how he would go about setting things up. It would be no problem for him, as I told him to believe in himself and understand there was a very large plan being created for him right as we spoke. We talked about divine intervention and when change presents itself, it moves forward by the universe cultivated by the angels and by God providing him the tools to get where he wanted to go. Glenn just needed to have faith that he was being guided by a much higher force.

Needless to say, he applied to the city the next week with the help of an accountant and got the contract for the entire park system. He formed the company with the help of his children and hired the staff he required.

The name I saw being painted was his new business name on his new white truck! It was a dream come true, he said, and he would always remember he can have a divine intervention again if he keeps the faith and believes he is worthy of the brilliant changes God brings to each of us when we are paying attention. And if you aren't paying attention, they may just shake you up a little to awaken you to the wonderful life path you are on.

Glenn was considered the master gardener for the city and Spirit considers him a Soldier of Grace, one of the loving entities who understands the importance of the need to honor the majestic trees helping make our Earth a better place for us all.

* * * * *

Earth is a precious place for every entity that God has created. There are so many creatures that man has never found and equally as many that have left this Earth because of the actions of man. Spirit works in all things growing here – the flowers, plants, and trees are all creators of energy. The trees are great energy receivers and when they are ill they lose their ability to absorb negative energy and recirculate healthy energy.

Man may have childhood remembrance of majestic trees, using them as play areas and embracing their safety and energy. Most people remember with fond memories a special tree they were connected to and go back to visit their old home place to see if the tree is still there. Many dreamers manifest their dreams while sitting under a tree, resting and waiting for their thoughts to float in as they mature. Some of these old trees have carried for many years the names inscribed on their trunks bearing thoughts of affection and safety. They are an energy force that transmits love into the atmosphere for all to feel on another level of being.

Honor these great emissaries for the Soldiers of Grace as they offer shade and protection for all who wander by throughout their long lives. Should man realize that your Earth is not getting larger for your lovely parks and playgrounds? Then man should be the gatekeeper offering care for these aging majestic trees so they will continue to offer the traveler protection from the heat and sun. It might appear it would be easier for man to just replace the ailing trees and landscaping but it is much kinder to your Earth to take care of these great helpers as they age and allow them to continue their job in grace.

Earth is asking to be honored everywhere. We are asking man to look around and not only help keep it clean but nurture it as your brother or sister. If man made this choice to care for all that is growing around him it would provide the world a much kinder environment for current creatures and humans, and even an opportunity to bring back many creatures that left because they could no longer survive in their environment.

Yes, all this needs to happen but being respectful of what is left is for ALL humans to care about, not just a few of you. One feels the energy much differently as you pass an unkempt area along the highway. It would be a kind gesture to ask yourself what you can do to keep the

Earth clean at this time. She is in very much need of this kindness which you can embrace her with at this time. An area of big, beautiful, green trees, grass, and flowers changes all creatures, children and adults in some way. This change man can share in could create a true energy infusion of cleansing the Earth, imbue every breathing person inspiration each and every day, and open the door for rebirth of all of the creatures who have left because of your Earth's condition.

THE SPIRITUAL DYNAMICS OF PHYSICAL HEALTH

It shall be understood that God has the same level of love for every creature that has been placed upon this Earth. All creatures and even plant life move and evolve in their own way in common love of their surroundings. Much can be seen in the ways that thought and understanding can simplify and provide for all of your needs. Silence and stillness in the body offer the opportunity for the mind to catch up, providing much improvement in physical health and mindful movement.

We mention many times in these writings how cells are affected by energy. The medical community is now realizing that people do not need medication for many health issues; it has chosen to open itself to more of the natural healing the world has used for thousands of years, dating back to the beginning of your time. Make it a practice to start and end your day well. Do not carry what you perceive as negativity; create a release that takes away worry and doubt, diminish their ability to cause harm to your body, and instead keep the door open for peace and joy.

You are your own creator of good and bad. It shall be a dance for all men to add much to their lives and you shall choose yourselves to adopt the beautiful new way of living. Watch and look for changes, believe they shall come, and it will be a short time until you will be told how different you look. This time the world is coming into shall prove to be a complete Earth shift.

Know Thyself

Everyone has their own story and not many get told, but this one stands out for me and I have to say I think about this woman often. Great reminder for me to channel my blessings daily.

I was teaching a class where a young woman in the audience had been in my awareness for most of the evening – Emma. I felt her energy was low and anxious so I was surprised when she appeared by my side as the group was winding down. She asked for a business card and briefly talked about a possible reading with me and then she just walked away into the night.

On the way home, I kept trying to figure out Emma's situation and then it hit me like a rock. I had been talking about how we need to look into ourselves for the answers through God's guidance and not be afraid to pull out that story we are hiding from ourselves – the real truth, not the material life many of us live in, but the real one buried somewhere deep in our mind and affecting our heart on a daily basis. I had a strong feeling she would circle back around to a reading with me in the future.

A few weeks went by before I received a message from Emma and her reading was scheduled for the next day. The minute I answered the call, I asked about all of the animals around her. She hesitated for a few minutes and I could tell she was getting emotional. She talked about a pregnant cat that showed up on her porch and the next day she had not only a cat but six kittens! Not having the heart to send them to the pound, she was raising them and it wasn't long before she had collected four dogs, a blind bunny, and a total of 12 cats.

During the first few minutes of the reading, I wasn't feeling she had real friends around her and when I brought it up, she spoke of her inability to connect with kids in school. Then when she had gone off to college, she just fell into the habit of working full time and studying continuously, which allowed her to graduate a year early. That had been her dream but now she was having a problem finding a full-time job that would pay enough to keep the animal kingdom she had adopted, her real family.

I knew Emma would be working before long but she had to settle a much deeper issue within herself that she had avoided for a long time. It was time for her to recognize her reluctance to trust, so she could make friends that would accept her just as she was. When we talked about her parents passing at an early age, she began to realize she really didn't have any skill for connecting with others on a personal level. She was amazed to realize how she had *passed up human contact for her beloved animals and had reverted to becoming a recluse when she lost her family.*

She agreed the changes were necessary and we set up a plan for her to take baby steps in connecting with total strangers on a daily basis. We discussed making a list of ways she could randomly connect with someone every day. Emma's list was to have at least two encounters by giving compliments and look for chances to help someone she could do a simple task for, such as opening a door or letting them in during traffic.

I could feel her face light up like a Christmas tree! She believed she had a plan that could give her the courage to grow into the real person she knew was in her all the time, but had been so afraid to let make the connections, mostly because she expected people would recognize her lack of belief in herself. When her parents passed so early in her life, she felt she had lost her only support team and actually convinced herself it was true. So for many years her days were full of "and so it goes," as she lived in solitude. Now there was hope for her, and we planned another reading in a few weeks.

When we spoke again, Emma had much to share about her changes, which just seemed to get easier as the days went by. She had made several connections in her part-time job just by smiling and making small talk. She had been out to dinner with two fellow employees and had joined a meetup group with other animal lovers.

Her biggest news involved her love of the animals; at her meetup group she met a couple of people who were looking for someone to take in some animals to foster and work with the pet stores to help with adoptions. She knew she had found her home and it led to a trip with a woman who worked with disaster groups to assist in rescuing animals and cleaning them up to return to their own habitat. She now was making money and presenting adoption and training classes at local pet stores.

Did Emma need to do a lot of personal work on herself? Not really; she just needed to believe she could bring her heart and mind together and empower her voice to become her true self.

* * * * *

Birth is when an empty vessel for the soul begins its work of learning the path and awakening the brain to the life it is creating for itself. The soul connects with the body at this early stage of life and launches its level of understanding and trust for this inhabited state of being. Understand, the process can be very taxing at the time of birth and even for many months to come, as this soul and body are connecting on all levels of existence for the future and it can be considered a fragile state. The brain is not prepared for all the information it is now receiving every waking moment. There are many levels of development for the soul to adjust to this new life, as it brings no memory of being in this same situation before.

The cells of the brain begin to activate themselves with the child's first breath of life. Their triggers become rapid, much like the brain works, all signals beginning to fire. It operates like the mechanical engine of a vehicle as it puts all parts in motion to spark the electrical current, fuel the engine, operate the transmission – allowing you to travel wherever you may desire to go.

The brain shall begin its job allowing the emotions to come to the forefront at this time through crying, mobility of limbs, and the appearance of sight. It is recording every movement of every cell within the body to assist all organs and blood flow throughout this beautiful, mechanical being. At this time, each parent and other humans present shall observe you as a beautiful gift from God. Understand, you are like a flower, just as a beautiful rose that appears one day and as time progresses opens to great beauty. Even though a flower is only to last few days, it still goes through the same process of birth and growth to show its beauty.

Understand that each rose shall not be exposed to every human, but its beauty attracts other species and helps keep this world in its growth pattern. The bees, butterflies, and other insects are attracted to the lovely rose and find the right food, thus sustaining their life by the one rose and they are very appreciative for this beautiful flower to assist them in fulfilling their jobs on Earth as one kind of God's children.

It shall be understood that God has the same level of love for every creature that has been placed upon this Earth. Their births are just as important as man's. And the flower is a food for man as it brings forth joy and beauty, allowing the emerging feelings to conjoin in the brain and promote stronger emotions of calmness and love to the heart, which are emitted back to the brain for deeper levels of understanding the feelings of love, calmness, and joy being experienced at such a time. This part of the brain structure can be assisted by all things of texture and substance to charge and awaken optimal functioning.

Every emotion a child experiences is collected and sent to the proper cells in the brain to become forever stored and assist the development of this human to structure its life. The same as when a flower flourishes and shines in its beauty, to be followed by another one on its way and then another, the small child undergoes and develops millions of emotions, thoughts, and desires to use in its connection with humans. This can be seen at all levels of the child's growing brain matter and it shall thrive on the creation of new cells to keep up with the body's growth so all organs attain their correct size and perfection for adulthood.

All creatures and even plant life move and evolve in their own way in common love of their surroundings. It is important for the soul to learn to walk, talk, and make decisions. This shall continue for the soul to reach each level of life – each electric spark within the body has a purpose to advance the soul's thoughts and the body's actions; sensations are present to alert the nervous system to protect every sense of love and accomplishment. These functions shall grow daily for the human to advance to a state of well-being if the soul has chosen this path for itself. This development shall continue throughout the entire life of the soul and shall proceed rapidly with decisions for each endeavor placed in its path.

Heal Thyself

When I read this section, I knew it was perfectly on point with what has been happening behind the scenes for so many years. While living in Arizona, my clientele was well-versed in many alternative health programs, looking to extend their lives by using all of the new modalities. Of course, these practices opened the door for a better understanding of the benefits from practicing meditation. Sitting in silence when we pray, we are completely in the presence of God; when we meditate, we are hearing God's guidance.

Finally, the medical industry is tracking the health benefits of these alternative practices, including diet, meditation, and other mindful exercises, and acknowledging their extraordinary contribution to reducing stress and living longer. Doctors have begun to add this new arsenal as vital components of responsible health care for their patients and today much research is going full force to stop the statistics of early death, a blessing for all of us.

This brings me to a reading I had with Christine, who had just started chiropractic school at the same time she was having serious difficulty with health issues and felt the career path she had begun was a mistake. She was constantly having panic attacks and overall aches and pains, so she was taking pain pills like they were candy to eliminate the constant agony she was feeling.

When Christine called me for the psychic reading, I could feel her nervous energy and feelings of despair. Getting caught taking the pain pills was her fear, that if someone found out then she would be a failure in her field. She was being taught how to relieve pain in her new school and should have been practicing the designated treatment for her pain, not taking pain medicine. Spirit shared a large piece of information with her regarding the stress she was creating in own body, which had no place to go but into her joints and nervous system. It spoke of the pores of her skin being stopped up from the stress and that was also the reason for such a bad breakout on her face.

I choose to use the phone as the vehicle to connect for my psychic readings, as I feel you get a better reading. This is because I am not watching your facial expressions and body language when the information is coming to me from Spirit. So she was astonished when I brought up her face breaking out, since she had not mentioned it during the reading, and she felt it really was a big part of her stress. She felt ugly and saw no way out of her predicament.

We talked about adding some meditation time and suggested a CD to use, as she had no skills or knowledge of how to start. She was also to create a few affirmations related to positive health outcomes to place around her house that she could review subconsciously during the day. She was to always acknowledge how grateful she was for having such clear skin and enjoying such good health. Finally, we spoke about gradually stopping the pain medication and making some adjustments to her diet. Being a student under stress meant that her fast-food intake was causing some of her issues, too.

The real shock to Christine was Spirit's advice about her chosen field for a career. Her father and grandfather, *both successful chiropractors, were pushing to have a third-generation chiropractor to take over the business. However, this was not a path she wanted to follow. Asked about her favorite childhood memories, the first one that came up for her was the ability to make money selling lemonade out in the front yard when she was seven years old. She talked about making flyers and passing them out in the neighborhood, offering 2-for-1 pricing. She saved her money every other weekend from her little career and was able to buy herself a karaoke set and when she got bored singing, she would play like she was a big executive putting on a meeting, setting up her writing board, and selling shampoo to a make-believe audience of her dolls.*

Well, a new marketing executive was born and pretty soon a book showed up to put her on track to becoming a marketing coach, with no signs of stress or achy joints. I must admit, she made a big change from what her family had planned for her career, but they also are her greatest cheerleaders. Christine is starting a new division for healthy eating and life coaching; I am sure she will go far, as she is still using the affirmations she used to move on from that reading several years ago. Rightfully so, words powerfully chosen by you can change your life on a dime.

* * * * *

The time is upon all for decisions that will affect each of you in the near future. It is a place of peace for health. You are going to hear more on the needs of each human as to the possibilities for receiving cures for any illness you may be suffering at this time. The medical community is now realizing that people do not need medication for many health issues. As we have said before, the wonderful body can heal itself by simply correcting the mind.

Your brain has the ability to conduct many electrical connections that can create harmony in the body. Stress is a single disease that controls every organ; how you are living dictates how long you will live. Changing just one small thing daily can add more memory to collect information that can help you achieve a calmer state. Silence and stillness in the body offer the opportunity for the mind to catch up, providing much improvement for the electrical connections to allocate the correct pathway for your cells to link together along the nerves and clean the current which radiates throughout your body. This shall open the brain cells to operate at the pace needed for good health and mindful movement.

This time the world is coming into shall prove to be a complete Earth shift. The collective energies working in your favor have grown in great masses within the past two years. The medical world has chosen to open itself to much of the natural healing the world has used for thousands of years, dating back to the beginning of your time. Much shall be delivered to each of you from the masses of media you are using today. This shall continue to excite us who are watching this perfect switch and helping Earth create a more harmonious existence; it shall be a dance for all men to add much to their lives and you shall choose yourselves to adopt the beautiful new way of living.

The Earth itself shall also receive some healing from this experience. Much can be seen in the ways that thought and understanding can simplify and provide for all of your needs. This is a time to look inward and benefit from the quiet time that you have had at your fingertips from birth. Meditation is a wonderful ritual that you shall find of immense help for all, finding a light that shines internally for each of you who will be ushering in this change. Natural healing comes in many forms and will become a common practice for all who are willing to participate in this new way of life.

Effects of Using Your Free Will for Goodness

The writing Peter and the non-physical beings have written here tells us the effects that can come to the body when we use our special gift of free will for goodness and how it can affect our lives and the lives of others coming into our space. As usual, they are putting the words out for me to share a very special psychic reading with you. The particular reading I've chosen for this section comes from a very different place of time in this man's life.

When I received the call for this reading, I had a feeling it was going to be an emotional roller coaster. The first question Danny wanted answered was about his fiancé Lea who had pulled away from the relationship about nine months earlier. He was concerned she would break off the relationship completely. As we got further into the reading, he spoke of being a bully growing up as a big kid with no friends until he started playing football. He then had more friends than he knew what to do with. Unfortunately because of his success as an athlete, he continued to be a bully after graduating from college and moving into a great career.

Danny's ego was so out of line that he was losing ground to maintain his successful career and in the process he developed diabetes along with high blood pressure. He kept asking the same question over and over: "Why?" How could everything he worked for and loved just disappear from his life? Needless to say, there was more than one reason for him to be in the jam he was facing.

Spirit's first words echoed the same thing over and over, with his life unfolding right before him; it was how he used his free will. Using a negative approach to his life certainly not only took away his fiancé Lea, but his health was going down a dangerous path also. The messages he received from that reading were just too hard for him to accept and he decided to keep trying to hold on tight to what was left of his life.

A couple months later, I got a call from him asking for another psychic reading and I could tell he was ready to accept some life changes in order to move forward. I saw that his career was about to make a change; he would be hired for something within the next two months; and it would be up to him to make the changes for his personal life to improve. But he had to believe it could and would happen – no more negative thoughts and blaming others for his misfortunes.

I asked Danny to consider a volunteer position with a local food bank and soup kitchen while he continued to look for work a few days a week. He was to start a journal of how he felt after each day and list at least five different personal contacts he made from working with the homeless or those coming in for a box of food.

Well, almost two months to the day, he called with a story that anyone would be in awe of. He had completed the journal as I had suggested; every day the number of people he spoke with increased, he was performing random acts of kindness daily, and he made a point to give compliments to anyone who would listen to him everywhere he went.

With his newfound life, Danny got a call from a local charity looking for a marketing position and was hired that very week. He still continues to work for the soup kitchen, now serves on their board, and is dating a young lawyer from the same city. He just got a program started for speaking to schools in the area about bullying, teaching kids to speak out, and he plans to expand it to as many schools as he can.

Danny's health has improved; he no longer takes medicine for high blood pressure and his weight loss allows him to control his diabetes with diet. Needless to say, he uses his free will for good, having learned that kindness and grace completely fills us up with buckets of love to share in every way possible.

* * * * *

It is a day of love for each of you as you awake. It is up to each soul to make a choice to live in the feeling of the moment and create a day of beauty, love, compassion, peace, and grace for each person they touch this day. It is not a choice of God's to give you the ability and take it away. This is known to you as free will.

Each of you has this wonderful gift and as you grow in understanding of how important it is to share and give of your soul to another soul. This is considered a gift to another if you choose to share. Your actions will help enlighten and usher others into a world of open heartedness. To understand this, man needs to feel the emotion of giving to another without any expectation of something back in return.

In the moment of exchange you feel your heart opening, allowing you to experience love from the inside out. The task of giving love will show you the path to come forward into a place of goodness. The expansion will touch another at the moment of this transfer and bolster their soul to continue this powerful energy of love on to another. This is the chain effect of love opening the body's cells for the energy to pass and grow within. It is at this time that the body fills completely with pure energy which enables it to begin the process of change. Just this process can help change a soul's mindfulness of sadness or anger offering another the chance to make a thought grow for themselves of goodness and worthiness. This shall begin a life of comfort for yourself as you are receiving as much or more than you have shared with a stranger.

We mention many times in these writings how cells are affected by energy. It is to be clear to all humans looking for the education of a body radiating pure energy that you will find enlightenment regarding its higher function if it is able to stay in a pure energy state. The body can rollback disease and create better operation for you to live a fuller, longer life. This pure energy flow can remove illnesses currently residing in the body and can also stop potential illnesses from occurring in the future. All organs and cells experience a complete cleansing at this time and operate with a strong force of wellness. It is the condition of love to open the cells of the body, allow all blocks to be removed from the organs, and hinder future sickness.

Try every day to pass this energy of love to someone, feel the change, and know you have gifted to another the very love you created, simply by choosing this task. Today you will begin to understand the ability to change your life. Taking stock of yourself is difficult if you have spent a lifetime in sadness and negativity. The changes we recommend will come in small steps but you will find they shall grow, allowing more balance of love and light in your life.

Watch and look for changes, believe they shall come, and it will be a short time until you will be told how different you look. This is a time when others may notice how rested you appear. Love reaps you great benefits.

Restful Solutions

One of the hardest things for people to remove from their mind is all of the negative and tough events of the day when the time comes for a night of rest. The anguish of sleepless nights is a sure call to me after a few days of exhaustion. Better than fifty percent of my clients suffer from this state of body and mind break down.

The first few minutes of each call when I give a reading is always the beginning layout for the season. Usually, their first words are "I am so tired, confused, can't think straight, and I need your help." Everyone is looking for answers but also a comforting solution proving they are safe and normal and loved. If they can hang up that phone and have a tangible solution that they can touch or speak, they feel powerful and in control.

No question, Peter and his non-physical friends have some powerful advice laid out for you and it will only take a minute of your night to take your worries and place them in the power bag for safe porting to the universe to carry them away and usher in opportunities to find solutions.

* * * * *

It shall be of importance to sit in stillness for a time each day, helping you gain knowledge of your journey, no matter how short a time it may be. Such moments are what we call "markers" – opportunities for man to pause and adjust a small part of his life. Markers are mini reviews you will use to proceed with grounding and adjusting your path with your free will to secure your emotions during this time. These adjustments may come in varying waves for you, even appearing to be useless time spent, but you shall find a treasure of emotions to assist in your growth, and especially growth in emotions that you perceive as slow to develop.

Not always has man chosen to become aware of this opportunity to spend time in contemplation of his growth and take actions accordingly in daily life. As you progress in your spiritual growth you will find this time spent invaluable to your balance as a spiritual being and you will welcome all messages coming to you during this time. Set aside a few moments of your day for this to become a natural way of receiving information from your higher self.

Then as it becomes night and you prepare to sleep, it is also important for you to review your day before you climb into bed and prepare for a restful repair of your body. It is best to review all of the events of your day and do a mental check of how and what you experienced. It is not for you to review and keep these thoughts in the forefront of your memory but to realize there was value in all the tasks you performed and let them pass. Take each one and pray in gratitude for what you experienced during the day, as it has sound benefit. Should not all projects and meetings played out with others have value? Make it a winning day for yourself.

This you shall call experience and knowledge. Thank God for the ability to work through any difficulty, should one arise for you. This is not for you to look at as a fearful experience. Thank God for the gift of being fearless and getting through whatever transpired for you during that time of uncertainty. When you thank Him for being fearless, you are already in faith of being fearless. Understand, this may need to be done many times, then a new set of issues comes to prove again your strength of faith.

It is much to think of this great accomplishment and understand you are now gifted with a new way to accomplish something positive and all things can come out well for you as your day of bonus. With this thought, remember: every day will bring knowledge and bonuses. Should you choose to see your day in this manner and retire for the evening, place all worries and concerns in a power bag to be handed over to the universe and thereafter forgotten, then return your heart and mind to positive events and accomplishments?

Make it a practice to not carry what you perceive as failure to bed with you. Go to this wonderful rest time with the joy of completing a positive day and to have created not one minute of crisis for you to internalize, as it is up to you to grant yourself good rest. You are your own creator of good and bad. You can have the glass full every night and wake up with your large glass empty and ready to meet your new day to get it filled up once again. Each day's glass will bring you joy and peace in not allowing yourself one spoonful of negative energy to begin its growth in your body. You have a wonderful machine to work with every day, to keep a calm state for body and mind to meet at the door to your soul. This is a great feat to accomplish and shall grow deeper every night.

Doubts and Worries

This call came in from Elsa, regular a client, and I felt there was more to her aching, painful back than she was complaining about. She wondered if she had been bitten by a bug of sorts. My response was a resounding no, as I saw a man's back turned away from her and felt it was permanent.

Before I answered her questions about a bug, I brought up the relationship issue I had just seen in my vision. Yes, she admitted a serious breakup was happening for her and she was still in a state of shock, but hoping for reconciliation in the near future. She felt she was blindsided by his method of telling her it was over – simply a text message. I reminded her of the relationship he had had before her and told her it was still open in his heart and that he needed to deal with that first. His feelings had just been covered up by being with her for the past year.

I asked about the dates and relationships she had had over the past twenty years, which had all been ended by the men. Her reply was yes, they all ended for the same reasons – she had been generous with each of them, helping them climb out of their pile of issues, after which they would leave her.

There is a name for this type of person, "the fixer." Many women play this part because they are lacking self-worth and do everything to hold onto the relationship – pay men's debts, dress them, help them find a job and if that fails, then support them financially. The women who choose these men believe they are going to be loved for what they are providing, and that they will never be left. Many of these men are just wounded birds looking for a place to catch their breath and when they get the strength to move on, it is usually quick and painful for the one left behind. Anyone can be down on their luck and many of these men, or women, really need this fix and mindfully make this lifestyle their choice.

From just listening to this information, Elsa knew it rang true for the situations she had burdened herself with over the years. There were so many changes coming into her life at this time, she wanted to call back for another reading that could finally help her get her life together. So we made an appointment for two weeks later and after I hung up the phone, I realized I had failed to advise her about her aches and pains. There was no doubt her worries were coming from stress which was causing her body to erupt in pain.

The cells of the body have pockets of congestion that can block their ability to receive nourishment and move the oxygen to flow energy that flushes out toxins; this was causing the pain my client was feeling. When I called her back a while later, she did not answer so I left a message about easing her pain and said we would talk further when we connected in two weeks.

The call came in on time; Elsa still sounded tired, said the pain was still there, and admitted that she had not followed through with the breathing exercises and meditation I had suggested in my message. I knew she still was grieving the loss of the relationship and asked if she gave any thought to a plan to move forward. Her answer was par for the pain she was having – vague. She just wanted to get past that and asked what her choices were at this time.

I suggested she sit down and get quiet with a paper and pen, take several deep breaths, and ask for her guides and helpers who had experience with relationships to come forward for her to feel their comfort and help her find the courage to write a letter. It was to be about the relationship patterns she was involved in over the past several years that she wanted to release with love and forgiveness and also do the same for herself. When Elsa was finished, she was to fold the letter, go to the store, and purchase a Mylar balloon that she felt attracted to, then take the letter, tie it to the balloon, and find a place she felt appropriate to release it to the universe. Certainly, not in her backyard!

When she was ready to start her release ritual, she needed to stand quietly and be very mindful of her actions and when she was ready, release the balloons and allow herself to feel the years of negative energy and pain she had experienced flow out of her body, removing any residue that was still hanging around her at that time. Then ask out loud for the universe to take all pain and memories from her body, mind, and soul to an open portal and away from her, allowing an instant healing. When she was ready to stop watching the balloon fly away, then turn away from it and not look back as she drove away. Affirm her new life free of pain and open to a new relationship that would be healthy and provide her with the love she deserved.

Elsa was so excited and felt she would start her letter that very evening. She promised to stay in touch and felt for the first time in her life that she was in control, would *no longer harbor doubt about her choices, and could give up all worries for a life of freedom. She looked forward to embracing positive thoughts of her impending love life. Elsa's faith was her guiding light as she now had the opportunity to have a lasting, bright future.*

* * * * *

Humans create doubts and worries on a daily basis. It is a human action that consumes a great amount of energy, and you are not aware of the need to release this wasting of time. This use of energy creates an opening that gives birth to fear. This is not always good value for energy; negativity at this time shall be very contagious and a chance for man to fail at their own hands.

Happiness is such a big leap of faith for many; it is easier to promote a negative energy than one giving you a euphoric feeling that allows you to move forward toward your goal. As you watch others who are successful it is a way to feel sorry for yourself and takes you further into a depressed state. Looking around and seeing other lives moving forward and feeling yours is standing still is a condition you have created at this time. It takes energy to remove yourself from this daily activity and put the work into making changes.

Understand that rest is a call for cell rejuvenation of the body. The cells call upon the body to slow down and create a mental desire and physical need to reach bedtime for them to start their work of healing. This is also a time when you take much to bed with you from the day. With worry and doubt, you turn a large amount of energy that you have stored up in the body into congestion in the mind, blocking a clear pathway to solutions for expelling this negative energy. The way you go to bed spending these hours will bond this energy and shape how it will be used in your waking hours. It should be said the human species naturally becomes a vessel for thoughts and emotions to cause this cell damage from stress in the mind-body connection.

It is important to create a release that takes away this negative energy and diminishes its ability to cause harm to your body, and instead keep the door open for peace and joy in finding positive situations in your life. Meditation is practiced by many of you and it is our hope that this practice will grow for all mankind to understand the connection to Spirit in this parallel life that is rapidly bringing the truth of our existence and love for all.

It shall be better to sit in silence when you feel a need to doubt. Silence is what brings messages to the mind and energy to the cells of the body. Stillness brings the inner voice to offer awareness of this state of mind you find yourself in at this time.

This is an opportunity to create a safe place to store daily energy from data that is still needed to create additional positive thoughts for a conclusion of success upon awakening to start a new day.

SOUL GROWTH LIFE AFTER LIFE

Many times the soul reflects on other transitions it has made in past lives, and feels it is being drawn to come back to Earth and gain additional experience and knowledge; it is not uncommon for souls to try many times to complete a particular lesson. Most souls have spent many lives with a particular tribe of human beings before. Life plans are created by each soul as they prepare for their next chosen journey on your Earth, and the lessons of any soul tribe are agreed upon before entering a reincarnation.

All souls have a memory with each life and an index of the development they have made during a time here on Earth or other worlds. Akashic records are for all human lives and very large, yet can be placed on the end of a pen without missing a moment of time. The information cannot be lost as it includes the DNA strands that follow each soul to eternity. There shall never be any loss of information; it is impossible for that to occur.

The soul alignment for gay and lesbian soul groups is not a new evolution, as this goes back thousands of years. These beautiful souls have chosen to help the world gain knowledge of

differing experiences with peace and joy in life at its fullest terms. Every soul has extraordinary love to share through knowledge and experience. No soul leaves without some knowledge advancement.

Chronology of Life Lessons and the Birth of Prodigies

Last year I had the opportunity to do a reading for a young woman who had twin daughters Ava and Alia, two years old at the time. She was concerned that one of her children was very active in music and painting, and actually scared of the extreme advanced level of her development, while the other twin was appearing to be slower than most children her age in motor skills and creativity. This was causing her to worry about their health and how she was going to handle the negative energy that was building between the girls. The younger twin, Ava, was in the terrible-two stage while the older twin, Alia, was operating on par with a 15-year-old.

We talked about the old souls coming in at this time to elevate the energy of the world and how she had been chosen to be the parent of this child prodigy. I assured her that she would be guided at each step for the good of this beautiful child, and that the younger twin, Ava was there to ground both of them into a normal family environment, providing emotional safety in situations that would evolve with Alia's unique, powerful talent. The twins were a gift brought to her for a very special purpose which would unfold right before her eyes.

One of the first things I felt with these two little girls was a determined desire to be alike in how they dressed and what they ate. When I said that, their mom laughed about their arguing over who was going to break the cookie in half so they both got the same sized piece. Now that is sisterly love! She seemed to calm down when she realized they still had a great connection, and that that was not going to change.

The other thing I saw was a lot of books and painting supplies lying on a table with both girls showing a high level of skill. I also wanted their mother to know twin prodigy, Alia, was shown in this vision reading to her sister Ava — the exact support the family wanted. I was sensing the girls would be home-schooled for a while, which would allow them to be together in a learning environment that could help unite them even more strongly as sisters, each going at her own pace and supporting the other with her accomplishments, especially as the older twin prodigy was advancing at a rapid speed.

This information just thrilled the parents and as time has gone on, it has proven to be accurate for their different levels of development. Amazingly, the parents have had the luxury of seeing the twin prodigy mentor her sister to the point that the younger girl has surpassed her age level. Both girls are involved in their local art school and have also become somewhat famous in their acting and musical abilities.

No question, these two young ladies have a lot of help from the other side, as they show kindness and love for one another, and the bonus here is Alia has graduated both high school and college, beginning her Master's degree in education at the ripe age of only 17 years. Never has she passed up a moment to help Ava gain her own milestones also. With compassion and understanding of her gifts and the responsibility, she helps her sister meet her goals and takes pride in the younger girl's accomplishments. You could say they are each other's rock and support system — the best gift any parents could ask for.

* * * * *

It is best at this time to explain the process of setting up life lessons for a soul and how this process plays out over time. Before birth, the soul releases all memory of world experiences from past lives, totally dependent upon its mother and father so there is no awareness of how they shall get food and keep warm. At that very moment, the life of the soul begins its struggle to depend on others to understand the meaning of love, compassion and trust. Let it be understood, no child is born into any world without the presence of God and guardians. There can be flashes of this presence that appear and many times children will still have visions when these heavenly beings are present. This shall continue until a child feels stability from the loved ones and beyond as living in a family of acceptance.

During the first three years of life, interaction and socialization shall port this child's personality and level of acceptance and discipline. The level of love and care at this time shall seat the roots for the child to start the lessons they have chosen to work on in this particular life path.

For a period of time in a young child's life, the veil of forgetfulness may be lifted so that a gift from a past life can be carried over. Many talents are so far advanced that people are astonished by their presence. Prodigies are born every day, extremely old souls who have used these talents many lives over. It is to be understood that these talents can be shown in a child as young as one year old. If a parent chooses not to recognize this talent, the soul will have assistance at this time from its godly guidance. These souls have started their life path and will stay on that path with great success, choosing to share their talents with the world.

There are many musicians, scholars and scientists that are living today through reincarnation, helping the world to continue its advancement with many of their own inventions from the past. In the coming future of your world you will see many more of these old souls reincarnating to assist with moving beyond your current capabilities. This has to be done to create a world of balance and peace. These old souls who have chosen to live many lives working in this capacity are teaching and training many others for their missions to create a more advanced and compassionate world.

As the soul advances, the teenage years are a conflicting period of time, for the soul has grown physically and is trying to catch up to their state of mental of growth. This is when the child can and will embrace its lessons of love, compassion, and trust through its parents or guardians.

This is a time when the soul begins the work of its life lessons. The dynamics of the home life and peer participation begin to form the data collected for this soul's self-worth. It is to be understood that no parent shall be completely responsible for a soul in choosing a negative self-worth. As we have stated in the past, the lessons of any soul tribe are agreed upon before entering a reincarnation. Each soul has a part to play out already transcribed for them in the family dynamics that will allow the child to work and grow in this current life.

It is also understood, no soul leaves the current world without some knowledge advancement. There are many reasons in the teenage years that a soul may choose a path that is worthy, and advancement shall speed up for completion of knowledge needed to become successful at an early age. It is also to be understood that there are many reasons why a soul chooses its life path early on and this shall not be known until much later in life, many times through a shocking revelation to all of their tribe, including themselves.

The real work that begins for a soul is in the next season of age in their 20s and 30s. The time then will be for lessons affirmed by the participating souls to begin their work of choice, agreed upon by the soul tribe. This is the time for all work to come to the forefront including karmic debt. This will also answer to spiritual values embracing fairness and how life shall be lived with joy and love, with a compassionate heart regarding others within the tribe.

The work shall begin to create a clearer picture for the next stage when the soul can realize whether the lesson goals are being met. The last milestone age of the work chosen for this lifetime can be a wake-up for the soul to begin accepting the uncompleted lessons and live the time left for this life. This is the season of many souls choosing to plan for their journey home without completing their lessons to their full potential. It should also be understood the soul may have chosen too much for one lifetime or was not exercising free will at this time. Many shall choose a life path that shall not offer the correct connections to the heart and values of others participating in the planned lesson, leaving another blank space in the soul's work.

It should also be noted that many souls complete their lessons, are happy with the outcome, and choose to remain Earthbound. There can be additional work one has chosen that is not in the soul contract yet is one's choice to continue to grow by helping others with their lessons. This is when many are feeling a pull and begin to remember tasks they performed in other lives. These times are capable of great creativity to be shared with the masses for joy and service to mankind. The veil shall again begin to thin and shall allow the moment to expand one's passions and previous abilities. This shall be different than the child prodigies we spoke of earlier, as those children were already chosen for their magnificent gift to the masses.

It is not to end this writing without noting the many beautiful moments of kindness and compassion that all humans express even at times others may miss, but be reassured some treasure from that soul shall reach someone and save a life while on this Earth. There will always be room for a kind gesture to play out for another at the end of life.

Divine Intervention

Wow, again. Peter and his friends have hit a compassionate nerve here. I am sure we all have encountered someone who has had a soul awakening they feel is a personal calling for them to change their life path and share their resources for the betterment of their fellow man. This happens more as maturity takes hold and a spiritual realization occurs that causes one's daydreams from youth to overcome the fear that blocked that direction earlier in life. Even if some do not act boldly when the idea for change first strikes the, it surely doesn't mean they won't visit that place again in their lifetime and make a shift.

Of course, I have a psychic reading for you on this subject, as there have been a few of these individuals I personally have had the honor to read for. I want to take the time to acknowledge those I've met and thank all of the others throughout our world for the work they are doing unselfishly. Hopefully, the writing here from Peter and his friends will let them know we are aware and appreciative of their presence.

Last year, I was asked to do a psychic reading for Charlie, who was looking for answers in regard to some opportunities he had received and wanted a chance to see what a psychic may have to say about them; he had heard of me through a business partner. I was so taken back with this man's clear energy and inspiration as he began to tell me about his desire to quit his CEO position, making loads of money and having enormous responsibilities for a major company.

He talked about having climbed the ladder and reaching his goals fairly quickly, but in so doing had missed out on a lot of his personal life, now finding himself alone and knowing he had a lot more in him than what he was doing at the time. While traveling one evening after a very difficult decision to downsize employees via lay-offs which would be over 10% in two countries, a feeling of clarity came over Charlie. He instantly knew how to save the majority of these employees for at least a year and offer them a chance to reinvent themselves with free education and counseling. When it was approved by the board, he set out to write his resignation – it was forfeiting his salary that would afford those employees the extra year!

So his call to me was all about moving forward and, being a man of such high corporate involvement, I was not sure he would really want to consider what I felt was the answer to his question. Spirit was definitely sending this man on a path of strong, divine intervention and it was not going to open all of the way at once. He was just on the verge of a great big, temporary move, more of an investigating journey of enlightenment. I spoke of a trip over a large body of water into an area he'd had some desire to visit several years ago, and the place itself had to do with water as well. I asked him to think of that daydream he was having about this area of the world and asked if he saw a lot of children.

Charlie was so amazed; I just love it when my clients have that light bulb come on bright and strong. Flying home about six months ago, he had read a magazine article and was so moved by the need in an African village for clean water, he'd spent the rest of that flight daydreaming of making the water available through a small capsule that could purify the contaminated water and save a lot of lives. Although, he admitted, many of these same ideas were already out there, he wanted to try to raise money from businesses to go beyond this and dig wells to make children healthier throughout the world.

I told him to give some thought to where he felt his experience would be best used and fill his heart with the idea to make others safer and healthier. We spoke of some other things that he should also consider for himself and made another appointment for 30 days out. When that call came in, I was the one amazed, as he was calling me from a small town in the states where he was wanting to see the countryside and check out areas needing assistance for children's education. We talked about his idea of helping with the water needs in other countries and that was still in the making for him, but he first wanted to spend some time reviewing what he could do right in his own part of the world.

The next time I heard from Charlie, he was traveling around the world, stopping along the way to do some sort of menial work to help and fill up his heart by offering personal assistance. Although he puts his money where his mouth is, he wants to remain anonymous, as he knows that is the true meaning of giving to the world. Meantime,

Charlie has met the love of his life who has not enjoyed the luxury he has experienced, and he says that makes it even sweeter for him as he has learned so much about giving from the heart, letting the purse come last.

* * * * *

The order of life plans is given to each soul as they prepare for their chosen journey on your Earth; however not all lessons, issues, and decisions are set in stone at the time of transition. There are many partners who have made the agreement to participate with you to acquire your lessons of growth in this lifetime and may help you alter your pathway.

There is always a possibility for any soul to choose to cut short their full load of lessons for their journey and elect to not work on their predetermined path at all. This is an option many choose, to create a clean slate for assisting others with their planned contracts. There are times when this type of soul may feel like a fish out-of-water, so to speak, and become the busy-body of their soul group looking to create a new pathway to salvage some of the duties they have carried over from another lifetime.

This can be seen by some as a lack of purpose in a soul's life, but their choice is to let go and follow their heart to assist others at such a time. Actually, realize this may be a correct path for this soul. Many who have made a choice to come into this world with a certain craft later decide to change direction completely to become a person of little fame, spending their lives helping the Earth regenerate a higher vibration of love through unselfish acts of compassion.

This can be a past life taking over at this time. Doing this shall give a soul a choice to ride out this life in giving back to the environment, seen many times in your corporate world where one has received great success and in a moment of deep reflection comes to a point of realization that they are not fulfilling a path for the good of the world.

There can be extraordinary advancements for any soul who leaves his own contract by simply walking away from a career path and stepping into a level of love that has no boundaries or misgivings about what consequences will transpire from this change. There are many souls living at this time doing menial work for the advancement of Earth's energy and growth. It is understood that any soul who chooses to live and work for the world's advancement is an old soul who is achieving success in other lives yet to be charted. Many who choose this path see aspects of their current incarnation they feel are more important, ways to better the lives of all souls participating in your world today.

Your world, as we have spoken many times, is in a spiraling depth of lost order because many are weak participants due to their lack of understanding the value of love and kindness beyond their own entitlement. This is why you will see a trend for some souls to feel the need to help your world acquire a kinder, loving vibration that will embrace all humans and creatures living at this time. To create this kind of energy growth, your world will need to sustain a much higher vibration. This can be achieved by sharing and offering love to all things growing and providing beauty, all the way down to a mere blade of grass. When man chooses to live and breathe this growth vibration, it goes within the hearts of all wanting to participate and shall be a contagious sentiment for everyone.

Does this actually speak of a soul walking away from his contractual responsibilities? And what damage does the soul create for his soul group at this time? Interestingly, a soul may make the decision to continue to live on Earth and break a contract at any time. Such an action can be expected and this possibility is reviewed with others in the soul group before all transitions of souls who are directly involved in each other's lessons.

It should also be understood that there are alternative plans already in place before a reincarnation to assure all souls affected by such a change will be able to continue their own growth with the small adjustment of removing that soul's participation. Another soul from the soul group will pick up that previous soul's job in this group reincarnation. This does not remove the original soul from their own personal reincarnation nor does it change the lesson plans of anyone else involved.

This soul's personal decision shall provide to those living in the moment an opportunity to demonstrate compassion and love without need for ego. This will be noted through the soul's desire to offer some small token of appreciation to the others for their work and to contribute on some level to their comfort for having adjusted. As we have said many times, it only takes one human with a mindful act of loving heart to helping hand to create change and growth for many from such an experience.

Return to Earth Transitions

I received a call from a client asking if I could do a reading for her friend, Carrie, who was really out of sorts in her life and looking for someone to help her find some direction. She seemed to have made several changes in her career, had just moved to the area, and was having issues getting settled. So I took a few minutes to sit and focus on this young lady and I saw a big stop sign; as I focused on the sign, it appeared to stay in my vision no matter how much I looked around the room. Usually a vision of this sort tells me that she could not see a future ahead and that the block to her appeared to be permanent.

When I asked how I might help her, Carrie was quiet for a moment and then began to cry. Life had been very difficult for her, leaving home very early in life to live with her aunt and graduating college with a business degree but just never really finding a career niche. She also believed she might have made a mistake, because recently she had moved to be close to a friend whose life it turned out was already full, and Carrie felt out of place trying to look for new single friends and a job. She had money to live on for about a year, but if she couldn't find a job then she would have to make another move.

Instantly, I saw Carrie walking a labyrinth in a desert setting which switched over to a large group in a classroom.

I asked her if she had been doing any spiritual work lately and she talked about some classes she was taking. I told her I felt a move was eminent for her and I saw an opportunity for her to start some kind of class for hypnosis and past-life work. She was taken back as she had finished two classes already and was going to take another class in Hawaii in a month, hoping to start a business with a classmate. She had gone back to school to become a physical therapist for a short while but just could not connect with it. She let out a big sigh explaining her reasons for wanting to leave her practice; she felt the work was not making people completely healthy again.

She was drawn to this idea of becoming a hypnotist for a new career after she had her own life regression a year ago. The longer she talked, the more I sensed she was about to find her connection with this lifetime. Understanding where her real pain was coming from for the past two years was sparked by her past-life regression and the more she had searched for answers, the more she would pull back because it appeared too scary and confusing.

I talked about the life contracts and life choices of the souls coming to her for therapy to begin their healing process. I spoke of her own mindset thinking if she healed people she came in contact with that it would heal the unworthiness she was feeling about her life. All would be good with her to move forward with her desires for a good future; it was not part of her job to change her clients completely, although she was there to assist them overcome some of their mobility issues and reach a certain level of health.

It was hard for Carrie to understand that soul contracts are directly related to lessons for each soul to work through to gain knowledge and fulfill goals they have set out to accomplish. Some souls may choose the lesson to be overweight or very poor in this lifetime, in order to feel the emotions of their choices and find their worthiness or resolve other issues that relate to making changes which may not happen quickly. The choices are theirs, not ours. This was Carrie's lesson: to find herself within her own soul's work. Of course, one of her lessons could certainly be to push herself into a soul's life that she would learn she does not belong in, and the lesson would be to know it was never to be.

She was getting some understanding of a soul's life work, but still needed to spend time processing the reading, so we set another appointment after her trip to Hawaii. I knew she would come back with a different thought process of her newfound life.

Carrie's call came in about two months after her original reading and she appeared happy and wanted to do all of the talking, so I sat back and just listened. She had finished her hypnosis certification and moved on to complete her past-life classes, but really felt she was not finished learning and her calling showed its path to her while she was in Hawaii. There were just too many things and places there that felt like home for her to not pay attention, so after a month she called an estate-selling business on the mainland and sold everything she owned, including her car. Now she was living in Oahu, working at a spiritual retreat, doing past-life regressions, and starting to teach people how to recognize their purpose and live authentically.

She was much calmer than the last time we spoke, with new clarity about what she wanted in life. She was experiencing visions for herself and learning to trust them for her path. There is no doubt Carrie has found a place to call home; she just listens and follows her heart, trusting information the universe is giving her. She knows more growth is coming and that is a blessing.

* * * * *

Many times the soul reflects on other transitions it has made in past lives. It then feels it is being drawn to come back to Earth and gain additional experience and knowledge, to understand where the ultimate purpose of life leads and how to repeat the tools needed to get there. Since there is no real space or time beyond the veil, ideas flash by and a soul is able to register each piece and how it connects to others at rapid speed. One may choose to speed up or slow down this task to ponder whatever main focus they want to consider at that time.

One may also feel a great need to help others as they prepare to join the main soul group planning to work together back on Earth. There are many souls that are fairly new to the spirit world and many of these have been chosen to come into the particular world you are living in at the present time; we shall not identify who or where they have existed before. Many souls want to go to various places in time and space to experience this process. Some planets are far more advanced than your Earth and then there are some that are more behind. The streets are quite busy in the afterlife, much like a daily shopping trip for food of thought and how it can best fit into the next transition.

The soul has a memory with each life and an index of the development they have made during a time here on Earth or other worlds. Not all decisions are followed as one may think of a soul's path, as each lifetime does not address every mistake or decision the soul wants to not work on; different issues are taken up in different lives. This can also mean issues you have agreed to work on may have been produced from multiple lives, not necessarily just the life you have agreed to come back and complete. It can be very confusing for many to understand about the soul's work, which operates much like changing the radio to various frequencies. This is done without much concern, as the soul's job here is to conduct all of the work that will give it the growth it needs to bring its lessons to an understandable conclusion.

A soul who is choosing to return to this Earth to complete the work of a past life comes with helpers along the way. The first thing a soul wants to make sure of is that they have chosen a human family to come into which will lend a helping hand for the desired understanding being sought – this is not just any family. Most souls have spent many lives with a particular tribe of human beings before. There are many connections they may have established from the very beginning and they are likely to have enjoyed each other's company and shared intriguing life paths along the way.

The goal of a human family may be to primarily help only one person, although the other family members can and will learn something. The real work of a family may be for a soul not even born yet. For a soul coming to work on its past, you may feel the need to be the first one born to set the situation up and prepare the family for the journey of that soul. There are many lessons or jobs a soul decides to work on that seem, from the human point of view, to be a very small part of a life. But it is to help another soul grow and understand their next move. All lessons are predetermined for a soul to come to Earth, and be assured there is a definite desire to complete and receive growth from each new life.

There will be more about this soul process in future writings. We shall provide information about the lessons that each soul finds, keep it generic enough to make sense to many soul groups, and clarify it point by point. Although this discussion will not be complete, we hope to follow it up with more intellectual details that you may use for your own life as we move forward.

Memories of Reincarnation

I have been blessed to have worked as a professional psychic for over 25 years of my life and have experienced some unusual and powerful readings. Many have offered me the gift of insight and every single one has provided knowledge that I carry forward to hopefully assist others in future readings and with these writings. I am grateful to share with you a remarkable reading I had with a young woman about five years ago. When she made contact with me, she asked me if I believed in past lives and if so, she needed to speak with me as soon as possible. This piqued my interest and I made the appointment for that same day.

When Elizabeth called, I could tell she was anxious and wanted to know if she could be developing her own psychic abilities. She seemed relieved to know that the answer was a definite yes, as we are all intuitive and capable of receiving information from beyond the veil.

The reading progressed into an account of Elizabeth's recollection, which began as she was recovering from a serious illness, of her birth in a previous life. She had received quick flashes of information that made no sense to her and they continued for many months. Each flash seemed to piece together a whole other existence for her and the location of this life appeared to be in Italy.

I had asked her to write down any future experiences that came up from the flashes and we would do another reading in a few weeks. The most interesting part of her memory of this past life was her ability to paint and in her current life she was not artistic at all, so she thought. She laughed when I told her she should try a few art lessons and just see what happens, as she had literally failed art in school.

Today Elizabeth is a very gifted painter, continues to hone her artwork, and has mapped a visit to that little village in Italy she has come to remember. Although she found no additional visions of that previous life when she was there, Elizabeth painted many of the hillsides and those landscapes hang in her family home today. She also has followed her current life linage and found she has relatives from Italy and France, as she continues to seek her spiritual path.

* * * * *

It is not for humans to have the same sexual preference in each life for all reincarnations. A person's life lessons do not always necessitate being a female or male for the next return to Earth. All lessons are prepared and worked out with the soul's group, and some decisions can be made as late in the process as moments before birth. There is no set timing, although the major plan is prepared far enough in advance for the souls to prepare their work with each other.

There are many souls who desire to continue working on the same issues in the next reincarnation. As preparations are being made, souls choose their paths and get assistance from a hierarchy of older souls that serve as liaisons for this major transition. There are many plans being developed and last-minute changes can happen, which carry over to the birth and growth of the soul.

Transitions are complicated to connect with the correct soul group and complete the entry back to this Earth. Each soul spends quite a lot of time looking over the Akashic records that hold a complete account of their reincarnations. There can be a large number of lifetimes and some lessons are repeated many times over, as in a single life possibly only one lesson was completed. It is not uncommon for souls to try many times to complete a particular lesson and repeatedly fail to create a positive outcome. This is all recorded for the soul with every detail, much like a family tree and an impression of the others participating in the soul's work.

The Akashic records are intertwined with multiple archives showing all participants including young and old souls alike. This history reflects others who are assisting the ones wanting to reincarnate. They are trained through their own lives to help others choose between love and negativity that shall help balance their return.

It is not the purpose of any returning soul to create a life of complete balance or punishment for themselves or others participating in the journey they have prepared. There is always a desire and a plan to come into a new life with kindness, compassion, and purpose for advancement. This is the free will of all souls returning. Some souls who have returned home and prefer to not return to Earth can stay in the afterlife forever. Others choose to come back and partner with someone for whom they feel a very strong pull, and so reincarnate with that soul.

The plans are completed in a meeting of many souls who shall commune to agree to the desires of all coming into this new journey. Understand that you may, as well as any other soul, have the free will to not return regardless of others' desires for you to participate in their new journey.

While choices are initially made according to a plan for the lifetime, an opposite choice may arise outside of the soul's contract. This happens many times if a soul halts their growth and selects a more difficult path, slowing down the lesson – somewhat like when you would take a vacation and it turned out not be a vacation after all. Many decisions the soul makes can extend the time it takes to work through the issues that were originally planned, sometimes creating additional obstacles to conquer. This is not to be considered a mistake but a larger karmic opportunity.

May it be said no soul can be held in guilt for not wanting to return for any part of the action that other souls want to participate in. They also have and show no anger or hurt for your choice at this time. It is understood by all that the choices made are wholly the desire of each soul and no one shall feel remorse for their decisions.

It is also understood that if one makes a sudden decision to return for another reincarnation, there shall be a chance that this soul who begins the process without coordinating a complete plan can change the outcome for the whole group and the work they intended to carry out.

This is where a soul can make a change as quickly as removing themselves in the birth canal. This can come through the soul's passing out of the infant body and not picking up at the time of birth the intended work plan that was made in the afterlife. It is to be understood that the transition can happen in an instant. This is a known possibility before the final decisions are made and is a move considered not to be made on a whim at the last moment.

Timing is important; know that it is not measured in minutes, seconds, days, weeks, months, years or decades. It is an instant. The soul is much like a computer that man uses in his world today with many operations focused on one point in time.

Akashic records are for all human lives and very large, yet can be placed on the end of a pen without missing a moment of time. They are comprised of the energy of the masses and electrical current changes as events occur. Words are not used but emotions and visions, to be read by the soul and those who are assisting in acquiring this massive amount of information. The recorded emotions as well as actions in these records can be felt when the soul reviews its many lives.

To record in man's world, this massive archive would be larger than all worlds. The information cannot be lost as it includes the DNA strands that follow each soul to eternity. There shall never be any loss of information; it is impossible for that to occur. It can be very difficult for man to comprehend such a conglomeration of information and this is also part of the data.

Transgender, Gay, and Lesbian Genre

Remarkably, this information coming to us now from Peter and the non-physical beings shows what a wonderful time it is to be living in this world today. We are embarking on an acceptance of each other's differences to reside in harmony, knowing that there are many out there trying to find a way to fit in, be loved, and show their love in return without rules from people with opposing views.

This brings me to a psychic reading for Danielle who was transgender, having had an interest in that lifestyle since she was four years old. Her parents, Diane and

Henry, were reluctant to accept her internal struggle to find where she fit in society when she made them aware of her desire to share her true identity and live her life as a young male college student. They had suspected her identity crisis early on, but chose to allow her to come to them when she was ready to determine the life path she would want to take. They were never opposed to this lifestyle; they just wanted her to be sure of her decisions and look for others who would fit into the life she saw for herself in the years to come.

Concerned for her safety and trying to protect her, Diane and Henry asked her to stay in the city with them while she went to school. When I received Danielle's call she had already agreed to try a school located in her city, however she still felt pressed to make a move to find the new life she so desired. She wanted to know if she should follow through and finish her schooling there to make her parents happy, or strike out on her own to follow the newfound decision to change her identity.

Interestingly, I saw that a young, gay man would befriend her in the near future and would be helpful in her quest for a more authentic lifestyle. This new friendship would not happen in school, but through a counseling office located in a hospital setting in a neighboring town. She would also make a very big change in her career options, one that Spirit told me her parents might object to.

Shortly after the reading Elizabeth met Scott and discussion ensued of his issues and how he had become involved in a group that she also might find would fit her interests. She agreed to attend a session and found herself very intrigued with such quick acceptance from other young adults experiencing gender identity. She felt at home with this group, almost like a den mother, and this was noticed by one of the faculty of the facility. After just a few sessions, she was having a conversation with the group leader and learned they were looking for a resident facilitator for the in-house bunch beginning their transitions. Next thing you know, she was hired and moved in the very next week, was able to enroll online for the same classes she was planning to take at the college at home, and was working in the very place she felt so accepted – mentoring and being mentored!

This gave Elizabeth the courage to move forward with love and acceptance in a safe environment for her own transition a few years later. I received a call from her, sharing her good fate of being on the senior faculty, having undergone her complete transition, and living happily engaged to a wonderful woman. Her last words of that call were very special as she expressed gratitude not only for her family's acceptance, but that from that first meeting with Scott, her newfound gay friend, she began to find the presence of God in every person and patient she has come into contact with since. Knowing you are loved and accepted when you place value in who you are is living your authentic self.

* * * * *

Transgender is a human term; for a soul it is a difficult transition to play out as a puzzle of emotions. Such a soul has had a life or lives in the past or concurrently wherein gender was not fulfilled. The desire to remain a certain gender did not release after that experience, and causes a duality in the personality of the soul running today's life. This is much like an embryo that has split part of the way but functions as one entity.

This crossover of intention means the soul is operating as a gender not aligned with the mind and body's hormonal cell connections. The brain and other organs have short-circuited energetically due to the overload of information in the soul's current body. This soul is also being overpowered by an attempt to honor your society's vision of the way life should be lived.

The completion of gender decision is not the goal of all transgenders during the lifetime they are currently living, as many fear the exposure to their immediate family and soul groups. Much can be felt in the mind and heart to assist this soul's decision, as there is no right or wrong answer for them at this time; we, as a loving entity, shall not support the world pressuring them to be like others at this time. To not accept the lives of our equals is a quandary for not just man but also your Heavenly Father who is watching this play out and seeing the pain experienced by so many.

There is also much to be said for the desire to undergo a complete physical change as the soul's desire to remove itself from influence of other soul purposes, to move forward living the desired gender expressing itself in the current life. This transgender lifestyle will alleviate this soul's conflict so it can grow and achieve the gender understanding it seeks.

It is said the soul alignment for gay and lesbian soul groups comes from a past life of transgender. These souls' births have completed the separation of both male and female genders, although their desire to live in the body of a desired gender converts to same-sex attraction. This is not a new evolution, as this goes back thousands of years.

The changes that are beginning to move to the forefront of society are for the reason to learn acceptance of all personalities. Allowing individual use of body functions will align man in welcoming these beautiful souls that have chosen to help the world gain knowledge of differing experiences with peace and joy in life at its fullest terms. This body and mind alignment is coming into prominence at this time for humans to more fully ascertain and realize the need to offer love, live a more compassionate life, and see that all must come together as one. It is not the desire of these souls to be different, as everyone seeks acceptance and understanding. Coming into your world with a different desire for human unions should be granted to all humans regardless. It shall be a new beginning for all to live and have a better understanding of a soul's ability to create uniqueness.

There is a purpose for these soul groups; they are considered very old souls who have agreed to come into this life and face the negativity to carve a pathway with their differences for all to live more harmoniously in this lifetime. Much is happening to foster acceptance at this time as your world shall face others within the universe that have lived closeby for thousands of years and shall soon be known by your world. This plan has been activated for many worlds and it is to be understood that man needs to accept all humans in their body or lifestyle. As we have said before, this shall help evolve this universe so it will come to be one and all worlds shall live in complete acceptance of each other and advance the appreciation of your and their uniqueness.

Lesbian and gay humans are not to be forced into a common human transition as ordinary souls and shall not be forced to change to fit within your world. Every soul has remarkable love to share through knowledge and experience. What a wonderful existence you can add to the world you now currently are residing in, if you accept all human beings as your brothers and sisters. It can be said you have much to offer in patience and understanding if they can be exercised with an open heart. The purpose of creating unique souls for your earth is not for negative feelings but a joyous opportunity for all to live as one, be God's children living in harmony, and share the world of pristine beauty that comes from pure love and acceptance.

THE GIFT OF DISABILITIES AND DISEASE

Illness is not given to punish any soul; be it understood, many souls of all ages have contracts based on developing disease. Therefore honor all souls that have your perception of disabilities; they are helping elevate this world to a higher level. These beings are given the task to fight for the energy of love in ways that others cannot understand at this time.

A child with cancer is a soul who has lived many lives here on your Earth and on other worlds; they have chosen to experience this lesson for others who are in their direct families and soul groups. A child with Down syndrome is not one wishing they had another body, but emits beautiful energy into the world and touches many souls on many levels. Their legacy is the love they leave behind on Earth.

One experiencing Alzheimer's has not finished their life at this time and their work can be moments of review. Living in silence is an opportunity for growth and some souls choose this to continue their bridge between the worlds of Earth, afterlife, and future reincarnations.

It is no different than any disease that takes a soul at a time that is not opportune for those left behind. Disease and disability are both soul opportunities and indictors for man to see where changes are needed.

Cancer

There have been so many psychic readings coming to me from patients with cancer and other illnesses that were not aware they had it until our meeting provided a scan of their bodies. This is not a tool I use very often with my clients, but when the energy is speaking to me, then I take the time to ask them to have their body checked out. Sometimes it has turned out that a disease was present and the client was able to catch it in time to live for many years beyond our meeting.

This particular reading is about Barbara, who had attended a class I was teaching some years back and whom I later helped with energetic house-clearing. Our first meeting lasted several hours and I asked a few times during our appointment if she had been around anyone in the past few days who had cancer. She said "no," and we kept working, but I asked again about her having seen anyone over the weekend that could have been sick – same answer, no.

As we were finishing up on her house plans, I decided I really needed to come clean with her, but didn't want to frighten her. I asked if she trusted me and she said, of course. We had known each other for several months by the time of this appointment, as I had been doing psychic readings for her over many months, so I said my prayers silently and asked "Will you do something for me and really make a promise you will do it as soon as possible?" She agreed, so I told her as gingerly as I could that she would be fine but needed to call her doctor as soon as she got home and make an appointment to have a mammogram right away. I asked her to trust me again and please make sure she would move forward with the check-up. We got ready to leave and I gave her a big hug and told her she was in great hands. I left that appointment feeling okay that I had not scared her and that she would do as I had asked.

Now again, understand, it is not my intention to put fear into anyone, but I felt the hand of Spirit on my shoulder and I was at peace with what I had said to her. Barbara was going on a trip to see her grandchildren and I knew if there was a problem she would take care of it when she got back, and when she went to the doctor, he would handle it from there.

Well, many months passed by and one evening, she called to share a story with me. So I sat back down to listen, knowing she was fine at that moment. She began with the discussion she had had with Carl, her husband, about my conversation with her the day I gave her the advice to get a mammogram. Needless to say he was very unhappy with the "quack psychic" putting "garbage" in her head, and had some other interesting things to say about my profession. But Barbara and I had developed such a bond over the months after the class I taught, that she felt I was trustworthy and called a prestigious cancer treatment center for an appointment the very next day.

When the doctor sat down in the room to discuss her need to see him so soon, Barbara began to tell the story of our discussion and why she felt so certain that she needed this test. Carl sat rolling his eyes like she had met a nut case; he was letting the doctor know he was just pacifying her. The doctor made no judgment, just took her to the mammogram area and told Barbara he would meet her in the same room after the test. Shortly the doctor was back in the room asking questions about me. He gently told her she had stage three breast cancer and he wanted to do her surgery the very next day!

When Barbara called to tell me all this, Carl was sitting nearby and he loudly stated he was very sorry for calling me the names he had and having cast aspersions on my abilities, and thanked me for saving her life. She said it had taken her several months to overcome the surgery and get her strength back to share this story when she could hold herself together, as she was so emotional about it.

I was actually shocked by this news; it just felt very surreal at that moment and I realized I had been so fortunate to be able to tell her what I felt from Spirit that day and to have her follow through. It was momentous for both Barbara and me. I was weak in the knees and sat for some time after that call.

Does this kind of thing happen to me often? The answer is no. I have been able to help two other ladies with the same issue, but I have to say it is not a general direction for my readings at all. The one thing I do know for sure is *that we are, any of us, used as messengers for strangers and loved ones on a daily basis, and I do consider that a beautiful miracle.*

* * * * *

Cancer, a rotting of cells in the body, is not a disease given to punish any soul. Be it understood, many souls of all ages have contracts based on developing this disease. Some that do not survive will live out very sad times that affect many of the ones in their family and others of the soul group with connected life lessons.

Some very bright doctors from hundreds of years ago have reincarnated to work in the field of cancer. Please do not disregard the talent of doctors practicing 200 years ago as not having the mental ability simply because they lacked the tools used with medicine today. These men and women have spent many lives working in their fields and many are coming back as a soul mission to remove cancers and other diseases that are plaguing your world today.

Understand that around every illness there are reincarnated doctors working for your world, having even spent lives in other worlds far more advanced than yours. These are the humans that are the great inventors, researchers of cures, and creators of medicines that are used today on Earth. Every moment there is a birth in this world bringing a new life to help cure cancers – your specialists of tomorrow in the medical field. Someday your world will be very advanced in medicine and you will be able to grow and replace any organ in an unwell body. You do see some of this work being performed at this time and it should be understood it will grow by leaps and bounds, eliminating many sicknesses and promoting healing over a very short time. Healthy foods will also come more into play for all in the near future by these very old soul doctors, as they have spent time in many cultures understanding nutrition as medical medicine.

This shall be a time of continued advancement with the acceptance of using blood and tissue from all creatures and humans. This is a standard in many worlds that are willing to have value of life, where there are no wars, no famine and no sickness taking lives at this time. They are willing to share their knowledge with your world when the time is right for man to accept it and not find it a means of control and destruction, but to show love for others and willingness to help all mankind throughout the massive universe.

Cancer has grown in your world through a lack of ability to treat the body as a temple for the soul and failure to give it the highest level of protection and honor. This, we say again, includes the intake of poor nourishment and other toxins known to man. Anger and emotions also play a large part in the growth of your cancers today. It shall be of value to each of you to spend a few moments of your mornings and evenings to process your emotions and use what you find in truth for yourself from your quiet time. If you notice just a small positive change happening in your mind, you are producing an energy wave for yourself that will help cleanse out the cells that are of no value to you at this time. When you have thirst, the right thing to do is nourish yourself with good clean water to wash out the debris causing your cells to swell and hold on to the very toxins you want to release.

You must take care to what is currently acceptable in your food and what is actually safe for consumption. The sustainability of your world is under pressure due to the destruction of your Earth's ability to grow good clean bounty for all to eat and process for good health of all cells of the body. Your soils and waters have been contaminated over time and man is turning a blind eye to the damage to this precious world. It is to be understood that your Earth and waters could offer so much help in providing healthcare and sustainable food where no one and nothing should go hungry.

There is a wave of new energy that is happening in a domino effect; so much will happen to remove the harmful chemicals used for all things known to man from the desire for convenience. You are seeing this come to pass in all parts of your world on a very small basis and you will watch this growth in your time left on Earth. There will continue to be an awareness of this movement to help; it shall be understood that you are already getting information from other worlds as the most evolved souls involved in this movement are coming forward at this time.

There are many species of unidentified creatures on Earth that will be of service to help with cures for your future health issues. There are so many creatures that are ready to shift into your reality, just waiting for the improved conditions of your environment and man's mindful participation in helping the world become strong and healthy again. There also will be plant life that will spring from the Earth and will be used as new bounty for medical research. While the oceans of your world could offer a tremendous opportunity for such rich sustainable life for all humans, it is of upmost importance for man to understand the need to treat these beautiful magnificent bodies of water with respect and take responsibility to clean and restore them to their rightful conditions as one of God's wonders. This will take time and every government and man of the world will need to participate to never allow the conditions to recur that are in existence at this time.

Children of Cancer

The calls that are most difficult to receive are helping someone process a terminal illness; each one pulls on the heart strings from my side of the table in any reading I do for these life-altering situations. This particular reading came from Jane, a seasoned client, who had just received the news of her niece, Megan, being diagnosed with brain cancer and heading to another specialty hospital for additional testing to get a treatment plan in place as soon as possible. She was calling for some positive words and really wanting to hear that a blessing would be created for this child.

Young Megan was coming up on her eighth-grade graduation and the world was just beginning to open up for her, according to her aunt Jane, and the family was devastated. She was a very bright and creative painter and her dream was to become a veterinarian. She had the heart for taking care of animals and helped find homes for stray cats and dogs, as they always found her in their search for safety and love. There was no question that this child had a very grown-up lesson to spread around for many souls in the months ahead.

It has never been my choice or responsibility to offer false hopes, nor to scare anyone with predictions of eminent death. I have always known from the very beginning of this gift that it does not include doing God's job and these situations are totally in His hands. My job is to offer compassion and comfort to help people facing this kind of crisis with love and understanding.

My first thought was that Megan was going to have a rocky road, but I truly felt she and the family would receive that special blessing from God. So when the call came in, we spent a few minutes in prayer asking for strength to come into the hearts of her parents, Stella and Randy, to bless them with the strength to face this unknown illness, and help their daughter know that a lot of control for her own healing had been placed in her hands through trusting God's love – to believe He would show her the path to her own lessons for this lifetime of helping those also in their time of need.

I asked if Megan had shown any fears of the illness and Stella said she had been very quiet the morning of meeting her team of doctors as they explained the plan for her treatment, realizing she would be staying in the hospital for several weeks. At that very moment, I saw a dog in a nurse's hat with a stethoscope around his neck. Needless to say, that vision was only a metaphor, but it was showing me there was a dog on the floor and I told Stella and Randy this dog was going to be a great help to their daughter. Stella just starting laughing, as Megan had actually asked if they ever allowed pets to come see the kids in the hospital.

I knew right then that Megan would be okay. I told them she would be taking over from here on out and would prove to be a little angel for the other kids in residence for their treatment. Her father asked what I meant by that and I reminded him she had been in training for this job for a few years from finding homes for the animals that she made feel safe. Little did they know, she had already found her strength on that hospital floor – Spirit was his name, a beautiful six-month-old Lab puppy who was a resident for all of the kids. The dog was the idea of one of the doctors and had little training other than giving these kids love and helping them find fun in their dreadful days of treatment.

The medical regimen was grueling for Megan and painful for her parents to watch, but as she began feeling better Spirit was visiting with her more and more. It wasn't too long before this young lady had started training him to sit with her while she read to him with his soft furry head on her lap and received a big lick for her attention. The pup would come every day when she was getting her treatment and lay by her bed until she started feeling better. Her dad was concerned she was taking the dog away from the other kids, but the staff assured him it was okay; this was his job and purpose.

About a week into this new bond between Spirit and their daughter, Randy called me to ask if she was getting any help from the other side and I asked him, "What do *you think?"* Not my usual response to someone calling a psychic for information, but I felt he needed to realize what was happening right before his eyes. He began to cry and said he felt a huge wave of love coming over him when the dog came into her room every day and he watched her monitors get better just with his presence. I then shared with him that yes, she had loving helpers and she would show her special presence here on Earth very soon to him and many others.

I told him Megan was in preparation for her own job that was going to show up in the lowest of times in her little life as a child of illness. She would prove to be a special being sharing something that would follow her throughout her life, that of a very old soul who was designated for many reincarnations to be one of God's Soldiers of Grace. There was some silence on the phone for a moment, a deep sigh of relief, and then the spoken words "Thank you, God."

Megan's purpose was beginning to shine out when she was well enough to go to the activity room, with Spirit in tow, to sit with the little ones and teach them to read to the dog. Even if they weren't old enough to read, they felt they had accomplished this wonderful gift for the dog, they began to show a stronger will to get better, and their laughter was contagious to all around them, making for a lighter energy throughout the entire floor.

There had been improvement in shrinking Megan's tumor and the doctors felt her chances were good if they could remove as much of it as possible. Her day for surgery was coming up, Spirit decided to set up residency in her room the night before, and she read to him just like she had done every day. Before they came in to take her to the operating room, she asked her father to help her take Spirit to the activity room and find a little boy who was doing better with Spirit there. Sure enough, they found him and Spirit looked at her as if he knew she would be back soon. She gave him a big kiss and told the little boy he was in charge of getting Spirit to teach all the kids how to read to him until she got back. He smiled and off she went.

Megan's surgery went well and when she was rolled into her room much later that evening with success of getting most of the tumor, Spirit was waiting for her and laid by her bed until she was feeling better. When she was able to give him a kiss and a few belly rubs, Spirit knew he was to go to visit the other kids in the activity room.

The doctors were so amazed at how this little girl and a strange dog had created such communication. Her parents had a different take on this bond and explained Megan's affinity for animals and her gift of compassion and grace to others who needed to feel safe, just like the lost animals she had found homes for the past few years, and what happiness she felt knowing they were now being cared for during their time here on Earth. This touched the doctors so much, they asked Megan if she would visit the floor when she was finished with her treatments, just so they could see her loving work in action.

Well, I guess, you have figured out the ending to this story by now. Megan did get well, has been cancer-free for six years, is going to veterinarian school, and visits local hospitals, including her treatment hospital with her own special friend, a yellow Lab named Angel. She has raised *money from her paintings to buy a few Lab puppies for some special hospitals willing to take on a pup in training to help children have a better chance at life in a new and special way. There could be a few more Soldiers of Grace walking the halls of these specialty hospitals helping children get a second chance at feeling safe and loved no matter what amount of time they may have here on Earth this time around, and I am pretty sure it's something they come back to do again and again.*

* * * * *

Since we have been talking about cancer, we would like to discuss the feelings and emotions that are prevalent in watching cancer grow in children and the times of degeneration and death of these truly loving beings.

Be it understood that God is not punishing children and making them suffer with such a dreaded disease. It should be said that every child is a soul who has lived many lives here on your Earth and on other worlds; they have chosen to experience this lesson of disease for others who are in their direct families and soul groups. It is also to be said that each child has a remarkable ability to show adult strength in the struggle to survive and appear to accept their fate when the time comes for their soul to depart your Earth. In watching this process for these loving souls at such a young age, you can begin to see some of the old soul wisdom they acquired from previous lifetimes come through.

They leave with gratitude in their hearts for the strength they were able to display and for being able to assist those whom their illness directly affected to experience greater growth and understanding of compassion. Their legacy is the love they leave behind on Earth. There have been great scholars, missionaries, priests. and many more loving beings willing to experience this type of reincarnation for the betterment of all humans.

Understand, for every soul who departs this Earth of yours as a child of cancer, many others survive from the tests and medical advancements that these deceased children participated in for treatment and cures. They emit the purest love of your God all around them and those in the hospitals doing the work to save these children are hand-picked for each soul group choosing to be part of this beautiful experience. Also it should be said that everyone choosing to work in children's hospitals have experienced many lives as doctors and nurses. Many stay in this field lifetime after lifetime so they may care for these brave little ones.

There are also children suffering from cancer in this reincarnation at present who as doctors in the past have treated children sick as they are now, to develop an understanding of the emotions these children go through during this time. These souls consider it a great honor to lie as an ill child and know that in a future life they will be more capable to make another child feel better or live a fuller life from remission. Because of their life paths, people in these hospitals are watched over by the most reverent beings selected by God.

Children of disease are special beings; each is an old soul coming as one of God's season of Soldiers – a Soldier of Grace. Please remember to honor them and keep them in your hearts, as they are all God's children, no matter how many reincarnations they have made throughout the worlds of the universe.

Down syndrome

Yes, I have had several readings with families blessed with children of disabilities. So this wisdom of Peter and the non-physical beings is on target at this time in our world changing toward acceptance and understanding our fellow human beings' choices of life.

I had a young couple, Ashley and Conner, call me for a reading about their newborn son, Jake. The doctor had told them Jake had Down syndrome and would not survive due to a heart issue that needed surgery which he was too frail to survive. They called for a reading with me for some positive words of hope and some direction. They knew of their son's condition before he was born and the doctor had warned them of his imminent, dire circumstances and a life that could be difficult living with Down syndrome. They had worried about Jake being okay as he got older if he survived long term, being accepted at school, and being able to live on his own.

Needless to say, the first words that came to me were this child would be a blessing. I could also see with all of the odds against Jake, he would nonetheless have a successful heart operation. His survival was a real miracle in many ways and definitely a product of divine intervention. He continues to meet everyone coming into his energy field with joy and love that is so contagious it creates a happy place no matter where he is. Jake steps up to embrace each stranger with confidence and projects an energy that exudes his heartfelt affection in every way.

Every single one of these families has expressed such happiness and appreciation for the gift of their Down syndrome child. Some have even been able to save a marriage due to the energy of pure love in their presence. One thing for sure, each of these children has come into this world with a special heart and job. Their contract is very specific and reserved for old souls.

As an aside to the topic of Down syndrome, twenty five years ago I was living in Scottsdale, Arizona, and a friend introduced me to a family raising their young son, Jason, who was born with Hydrocephalus, commonly called "water head babies," complicated with Cerebral Palsy affecting his speech and motor skills, as well as paralysis on one side of his body from a stroke. Due to the pressure on his brain, Jason has been legally blind since birth, lived with a shunt requiring multiple replacements all of his life, and suffered numerous life-threatening seizures.

Jason did not walk or talk until he was four and a half years old, but used telepathy and sign language to communicate. He never understood that he was handicapped, believing he could do anything he wanted in life as long as he worked hard. His parents, Judy and John, had a wonderful sense of humor that they blessed him with, and through his many friends and family Jason has grown to be a very empathetic and compassionate young man.

They say when you are ready your teacher shall come, and I definitely believe I was blessed to experience this friendship and have the opportunity to get to know Jason as a truly joyful child who knows no boundaries from his disabilities. Jason has been one of God's teachers all of his life and I am so glad I have had the chance to be a friend and feel the love he emits each day without any reservations for his lot in life.

Today Jason is 34 years old, has conquered many health issues and remains a positive, loving young man who doesn't see disabilities but opportunities to live his life to the best of his ability, offering each person who comes in contact with him a mindful gift of what should be important to each of us, love. Simple to say but hard to keep in our hearts in today's world.

* * * * *

You asked earlier about children with health issues from birth, as they begin their fragile lives in this world. We will cover a variety of health issues within these writings and today we would like to talk to you about children born with Down syndrome.

It is not to make a child suffer or for a parent to mourn their desire for a healthy, vibrant child. It is an agreement made by the child's and the parents' souls before this reincarnation. There are many on Earth who do not believe in or understand reincarnation so let us say God does not put suffering on any soul regardless of whether or not they have completed their life contract, such as purposely giving you a child born with any disability. It is totally up to you to bring forward any lessons, health issues, or the wish to help a soul choosing to elevate love in the world by using a body of special needs.

It is not our desire to give you information for how to heal a soul's decision at this time but it is our desire to help you understand how important it is to experience a special needs child growing up to become an adult able to have such a magnificent position of utterly pure love in the world and in a small way to touch many souls. They are not after sympathy but are doing their jobs with joy and peace. Many stay a longer time to create love in a community or region.

A child with Down syndrome is a happy child, not one wishing they had another body. Their happiness emits beautiful energy into the world and touches many souls on many levels. This special-needs spirit has the ability to lead whatever life his parents will allow. The parents or guardians can use their free will to allow this special one the freedom to live and learn at their individual level; we see this beautiful soul living a life of joy and brave spirit if allowed. Remember, this child will be happy and will accomplish much if encouraged to do so. Not to say they don't create their life by free will, but we are speaking of when these children are very young. If the parent or guardian has guilt attached to the soul born into this beautiful energy that chooses to live this life in a different way from others, the guilt or anger about this condition can be nothing more than a lesson for the parents to learn from.

Any soul can grow and become whatever they shall desire; they know the world can be there for them and use their bravery to reach out to God's light and energy. It is not the soul's desire to create any negative thoughts or blame for their parents. They want them to rejoice in their choice of life. They are very old souls who choose to come into your world with perceived disabilities. They are very aware of the pure energy they are creating just within their presence. Allow these special souls to receive your love when you come upon them, as they intend to use their condition to share this special energy.

It is very admirable for any soul to take on this job on as a Soldier of Love, one of the six Soldiers we speak about. This being is given the task to fight for the energy of love in ways that others cannot understand at this time. They work very hard and make every moment count to create a thought process for humans to be kind and full of love on many levels. We all want to be loved and experience joy in our lives every day; this is the life of a Down syndrome child. The world is blessed to have such beautiful, kind spirits working among us.

Regardless of a soul's purpose regarding past-life health issues, the current body can create the ability for some past life cells to become active and experience their work in this lifetime. Every soul has experienced a major illness in one of their past lives and it is brought into this life in a way that the body will experience a small wave of memory. The cells within each new body are in sync with the soul and they shall interconnect, such as getting a tank of gas to run the distance. Some residue of the illness remains in the current body, regardless of the soul's desire to create health in this lifetime.

There is a television show many humans watch called Dr. Oz; this is an example of past life occupations. He is a man of gifted with teaching and being a heart surgeon. The trauma of grave health issues we gravitate to in a lifetime are from our own past and become the springboard for skillful careers today. This man is reaching the masses in a good way for many who have the need to hear him.

There are many skilled humans who are doing their work in a multitude of careers that are currently reaching the masses, and many others will come forward to realize they also have the skills to do the same. This is why humans write so many self-help books; many are very successful reaching just the ones that they need to. This is the work of the universe at its best. There are those operating in this world as teachers who have spent many past lives teaching. Many choosing to do this work are very old souls and we are grateful for their return to continue this blessed work. These times are actually for the elevation of patience and understanding, and diseases and disabilities are used to awaken people one by one.

Therefore, honor all souls that have your perception of disabilities; they are helping elevate this world to a higher level. Small pods of this energy create much larger areas and touch thousands, without a soul of this work needing to move around the world many times to complete this action.

Alzheimer's Disease

I cannot tell you the number of clients who are dealing with a family member who has this disease. They struggle with guilt regarding the inability to care for them at home, wanting to keep them close as they slip away. It can be a very long journey saying their goodbyes and some still deny the process.

I remember one specific reading for Judith who was quite young when she developed Alzheimer's and received information she would not have a long time before her full transition into this illness. She was divorced with teenagers and enjoyed the love of both parents and sisters. Afraid to be a burden to her family and especially her children, she asked for some direction in her process.

One of the first things that came up in that reading were two very large books with stacks of pictures on top of them, a tape recorder, and several beautiful boxes. The moment I saw the vision of the journal it became very clear that this would be her next step if she chose to listen to her loving spirit guides.

They were showing her a way to give her family the gift of wonderful memories in making picture albums for each of her children with fond thoughts of their experiences noted by the pictures. She also decided to make special engravings on her fine jewelry to be left behind for her daughters. The family members each received a pretty box with their treasures of pictures and trinkets from her life. She then wrote each a letter about her experiences and how she wanted to be remembered, and recorded her words for the girls to always remember what her voice sounded like.

The only thing left for her was to plan her funeral and she became very explicit on how and where her ashes were to be spread. Judith listened to the messages from her divine helpers and followed her heart to create a celebration for when she was gone, giving her family the freedom to grieve without the heartache of what to choose for her death rites.

When I found this writing in the work Peter and the non-physical beings, I was thankful for the opportunity to understand this disease process and share this with you.

* * * * *

Souls begin their journey the moment of birth and never finish their growth until leaving Earth through death. It is much said that a soul of Alzheimer's does not have a life nor do they create much growth for themselves as the disease progresses. Tonight we shall talk about Alzheimer's and the journey for everyone close to that soul.

Many families and friends feel they are being left behind and become frustrated at times, as this disease is a very difficult one to work with. It creates guilt in many left behind watching their love one slip away without realizing they are very much a part of the purpose for the soul choosing to prepare for the journey home in this way. All decisions to experience the trauma, sadness, and support were made within the soul group before this reincarnation. You will find it also gives humans an opportunity to realize life is for a short period of time, and the importance of giving and receiving love to another.

Yes, the body does begin to break down as it shall when the connection is being separated. One experiencing Alzheimer's has not finished their life at this time and their work can be moments of review and living between the worlds they already know. Much can be said for a soul who appears not to be attached to anyone or anything during this disease process. The ones who are left behind have difficulty reacting to this, without knowledge of the emotional work that is being continued by the soul for its time left on Earth. Know that no punishment is imposed on the soul afflicted with Alzheimer's. This is like any process of advancing diseases and the ability to be fully engaged, whether it is through the body breakdown or in sickness.

Living in silence is an opportunity for growth and some souls choose this to continue their bridge between the worlds of Earth, afterlife, and future reincarnations. Although surroundings are not recognized, the soul is living and processing in another time and space. It is to be understood that life sometimes can be difficult to complete all lessons the soul had planned for in this reincarnation. At this time a soul is given an opportunity to remove itself from Earth and use the opportunity of silence for its review of how the lessons are playing out and reflect accordingly.

The family and loved ones watching this illness are forced in their minds to process their own lives and consider the paths they have taken during their time on Earth. This gives you a rare opportunity to conduct your own soul review while still on Earth. It shall give any human the opportunity to adjust their own path during this time, helping their loved one during this challenging time in the life and death process. This is a promise made to all souls directly involved in this journey to complete in life. There is much to learn about anger, fear, guilt, and sadness, as these are the emotions that have ruled the souls in everyday life with a disease such as Alzheimer's. This process shall gift those left behind to complete the healing process and continue their life in fulfillment of love and compassion.

This disease appears very sad to humans but it is no different than any disease that takes a soul at a time that is not opportune for those left behind. Try to process this in each of your lives in some way to help prepare for life changes in your own future. All that you experience in this process is the gift of growth and a life well spent.

PHYSICAL AND SPIRITUAL SENSES

There will come a day when the senses will all be understood as avenues of communication for the purpose of dialogue. Know that not only can man depend on the other senses should one no longer function; the physical body senses can be replaced for each human in an enlightened state with the spiritual body senses of the mind's eye. Every human or creature has the ability to heighten any and all senses God has gifted them with during their lifetime to the level of Spiritual Senses. The more man shall work with the Spiritual Senses in pureness, the third eye shall perform the ability so nothing shall be hidden and all endeavors shall be available to the souls of this universe for the greater goodness of your world.

Each sense is an immense gift of love, being connected to the heart, enabling man to feel the beauty of the world and find opportunities to extend love to one another. The senses help people become aware of non-physical beings, including loved ones who have departed and want to reconnect. Many gifted humans are able to use their senses for communication with those living in the afterlife, offering comfort

to others for the loss of their loved ones and the guiding messages each soul can experience if desired. Sit in stillness and listen for the silence, as that is when you will hear the most.

The Basic Senses

This particular section brings to mind many readings that are worthy of sharing the awareness they lend to this beautiful writing of my friends. I hope you find them as powerful for you as they were for me, as they continue to leave an imprint on my heart and perhaps will do that for yours, too.

* * * * *

God has designed your body to be a magnificent gift to each new soul upon its journey to your Earth with the wonders of sight, hearing, touch, smell, and taste. The body has been thought out so completely that it is adaptable even without all of its senses. If any sense breaks down then another part of the body shall become available to assist with its own precious ability to compensate for how that sense allows you to use your physical world. These beautiful gifts and many other features of God's greatness are completely designed to enable life here on your world as it has been on many others, totally dependent upon His wonders for survival. It should be understood that all worlds have this innate ability, this communion with God through his gifts, and many are so far advanced that thoughts are not needed; simply by their presence are souls instilled with such rewards. The spiritual body shall also have all of the five senses and as you evolve to a higher level on your path; the Spiritual Senses shall be inwardly active and operate at the highest good for man and creatures calling your Earth home. We shall be speaking of both the physical and the spiritual body senses.

Sight

I received a call one day from an old friend who thought it would be helpful to gift a reading to Melissa, going through a very rough patch in her life, as she was facing some health challenges. I made the appointment for the next day and as the morning wore on I knew it would not be an easy reading, because I felt the need to say her health was something she needed to take care of and I knew I would get a lot of push-back. I think I have said before in this book, I am not a doctor and do not play one, but I do voice words of encouragement for someone to get help when the need comes up and Melissa definitely needed help.

I spent most of an hour in silence before her call; I felt such an urge to be on target with her needs and hoped the reading would go well. Her call came in right on time and she seemed to settle into the reading pretty quickly with a list of questions. She stuttered as she began to read her list and I knew in that moment she was having trouble seeing it. When I asked Melissa if she was going blind, she began to cry and became distraught, so I ended the reading and spent a few minutes just talking, trying to create a sense of calm for her. I knew the reading would happen later, but I just could not hang up the phone and leave her in that state.

I asked if she had any family she was close to and she let me know it was a subject she didn't want to talk about. I asked about close friends and her answer was pretty much the same. And although we shared a mutual friend, she chose to just shut down. After several minutes of casual chatter, she revealed she had just lost her mother to cancer, the one person who had really been her rock, and now she felt very alone, as she had no other family. She was sure her issue was cancer also and simply did not want to know it was taking her life right then. The reading continued before I realized we were really deep into her issues and Melissa was asking some of those questions she couldn't see on the paper she had taken the time to write out.

Her mom had left her a house she did not want, as it was her childhood home in need of some work, as well as a good-sized nest egg that would give her the freedom to get help with her health and decide where else she wanted to live. I asked why the ocean was so special to her and the answer was very telling of her journey ahead. She had always wanted to have a condo on the beach, a place to feel the ocean breeze on her face and hear the wonderful calming waves as the tide would change with the evening sunset.

Her questions all seemed to be referencing a fear of death rather than looking forward to a change of scene, mostly knowing her life was going to pass by and she would not be able to make up for lost time. I assured Melissa she was going to be around for a while and that it was *really necessary for her to go to a doctor and find out her condition. We talked a while longer and lastly I asked if she ever wanted a dog in her life. That was a big "no," as a dog meant responsibility and she was not interested. When the call ended I laughed to myself, as I knew a dog was out there with her name on it!*

Melissa called about six months later for a follow-up. She had gone to a doctor and found out she was definitely losing her eyesight, as she was diabetic and it was quickly taking her vision in one eye and she was showing signs of loss in the other eye as well. She told me that she was very grateful for the reading because without it she would not have gone to the doctor and would have lost her sight in both eyes quickly without the medicine she was now taking for the diabetes.

She was very excited to tell me she had sold her mother's house and bought a condo on the Georgia coastline, right on the beach. I was so happy for her, telling her how she had walked through her fear and found a pot of gold on the other side. She laughed as she agreed she really did get a pot of gold, as a matter of fact, whose name was Hope — a Golden Retriever, trained seeing-eye dog! The new love of her life was not only her companion but her family and social director. She had met so many new friends and had begun catching up on many things she had missed. She was putting a book together of her childhood poetry and working on a new hobby of photography. Although Melissa knew she was going to be blind someday, she would always be able to see her photos in her mind's eye.

* * * * *

The first sense that the Earthly body is very aware of is that of sight. Although the soul and body can do without this gift, it does have a tremendous role in the everyday work of man and his sense of direction. The physical body is mindful that without this sense it would not feel the beauty of the world as much, especially the seeing of other souls as they exist here on Earth, as the eyes are directly connected to the soul.

There is love and kindness generated by this sense and if the soul's body is in its correct state then the treasure it shall perform in the mind is to sync with the heart and connect to the arms for embracing another human or creature for the expression of such wonderful emotion and to the legs for being first to commence moving toward another soul or creature. The sense of sight shall offer the unselfish ability to assist any soul in need and to receive comfort in turn for extending this precious energy of love to another.

It shall be understood that the physical eyes are important but man can depend on the other senses should sight no longer function. Blindness can be considered another kind of a gift to those who are enlightened and improving the world with their love and eagerness to serve others. Know that this physical body sense can be replaced for each human in an enlightened state with the Spiritual Sense of the mind's eye; the spiritual body sense shall be able to emit love so that you may still make your way forward and all can be seen wherever sight shall be needed, even for what has not been shown to you in the past. The more man shall work with Spiritual Senses in pureness, the third eye shall perform the ability to view all of Earth's beings and creatures sharing the world's beauty wherever sight shall desire to go in grace. Nothing shall be hidden from this Spiritual Sense of sight and all endeavors shall be available to the soul of this universe for the greater goodness of your world.

Touch

A message came into my office requesting a psychic reading from Marcia, a young lady who was at a crossroads with work and wanted to find another place to live, as she had been in the same area all of her life. She talked about feeling a huge pull to the West Coast although she only knew a few people from school living there. She had endless thoughts from an·exciting dream about moving that seemed to come at least three times a week, and found herself doing really strange things so that her friends were embarrassed to be with her.

Well, there was no mystery here, so I was ready to hear all about her dreams. When she called and I got into her energy field, I knew she was on her path of spiritual enlightenment and a move was certainly imminent, as she was about to break open to a whole new direction of developing her sense of touch, better known as a clairsentience – she was becoming a clairsentient being!

She wanted to ask about the uneasy feelings she was experiencing when she got in large crowds. Marcia found herself just walking up to people and saying things about their lives that would be very overwhelming for her and them, as what she said rang true for these people. She had met a few that wanted to know more, but many became scared and asked her to go away. She found herself in a quandary as to how she had no control over her actions; it was happening more and more and just getting to be too much. The tough part about this newfound power was that her friends and family did not want to be around her anymore when she went out to the mall or even the grocery store, afraid they would get into trouble one day if someone called the police on the "crazy woman." I had to laugh a little, as many new clients report this reaction.

I asked if she was finished with her schooling and sure enough, she was employed as a physical therapist for a large orthopedic group. She spoke of her original dream of working in sports medicine but becoming a therapist was as far as her purse would take her education and she was okay with that. Since she had started her new career, she was dealing mostly with sore necks and sprains, but with her new insights she was having difficulty limiting her work to just their current injuries.

It was time to share the meaning of what was happening and where it was taking her. When I started telling her she was already healing people using her newfound ability, she was so relieved to learn she actually had the gift of touch and that it would allow her to grow into a whole new way of living and viewing the people she was choosing to work on. Marcia was also in wonder to have such a gift from God and know she was being guided on her path; it gave her a new mindset with an open mind and heart. I knew there would be more to come in the very near future!

The move I saw for her was definitely to the West Coast, although she had some work to do to get there and be able to support herself. We set up another appointment in 60 days to see how far she had come with the tips I shared with her to control her urges to get into others' space without their approval or desire for the information she was hoping to reveal. The number one rule for Marcia was not to share or touch another person without their consent.

The next call came on the date of her 60 days with so much to tell me that her excitement was hard to contain. She indeed made the move to San Diego and got a part-time therapy position with a group of holistic doctors, where she had become a much sought-after therapist for the clientele, and was also working on-call for an orthopedic medical group. The holistic team was involved with some meet-up groups where she had found a small healing gathering and was offering her skills, being mentored by a long-time healer living in the area, and showing much promise for herself in the world of healing the body and helping the soul, one touch at a time.

She was certain God had given her the purpose for this transition. Seeing the pieces that fell at her feet to make the move possible was life-altering. No doubt, Marcia knew her sense of touch was God's hand gently pushing her forward into the world of living her gift and caring for all who would make their way into her space of love. And the loving energy of San Diego would make sure it was going to be home to her for a long time.

* * * * *

The sense of touch is another immense gift of love for those who come forward and flow around you at all times. As it exists from the heart, touch can be sensed on many levels if man remains open to feel this beautiful loving energy that can feed the soul and warm the hearts of others for a life of caring and protection for all that is around. Touch can be used to find pockets of negativity from painful experiences and correct those with healing practices available to all souls and creatures of the universe. It allows the body to observe and maintain a proper healthy state through the activation the brain's electrical current to control the internal heating system, enabling the soul to measure and manage cold and hot temperatures for comfort.

Every human or creature has the ability to heighten any and all senses God has gifted them with during their lifetime to the level of Spiritual Senses. For the sense of touch, this elevation shall especially guide you to using your energy for bringing love and comfort to another soul or creature, and refusing to accept the negativity that can otherwise diminish your use of touch for a lifetime. Touch is an intuitive ability within all humans as they are gifted with it at birth to sense danger and when they need protection, as well as to know the importance of doing goodness and making decisions that assist and comfort others. It helps the brain keep the cells of the body operating at a healthy level for proper functioning and being mindful of the need to be in service.

Hearing

This reading actually materialized by accident. I was at the Chicago Airport on a lay-over due to bad weather waiting for my final flight to visit family over the Christmas holiday. My Kindle had lost its power and I couldn't find a space to charge it other than in the adjoining bar, where I took a seat at one of the small tables next to a wall plug for charging it. The place was filling up quickly and I saw a woman who was overloaded with bags and a carry-on hanging from her shoulder. I motioned for her to come sit with me and she looked like she had just found her best friend.

Lorie talked incessantly about not wanting to make this trip home because she had lost both parents over the summer and her sister, Heidi, was in the last stages of cancer. She began to cry, as she felt so much anger that her life was spinning out of control. She had suffered another loss when her husband left her a few years ago, and was now trying to get her life back on track for herself and her daughter. She felt pulled by her brother and another sister to move home so they could be together as they faced the pending loss of Heidi. It was more than she could take to feel any more guilt than she had already suffered through.

I could tell she was really facing an overload and I felt urged to share a message from her dad whose name was Dale, so I asked if she believed in life after death. She said it was not something she really thought about that much, although she hoped there would be a chance to see her family again. Then I asked if she had Dale's watch with his wedding date engraved on the back. She was shocked and pushed her coat sleeve up to expose his watch. I told that he was doing fine and so was her mom, Evelyn, and they were waiting for Heidi to cross, as they would help her make the transition. Her dad told her to consider continuing to live where she was and just make more time to see her siblings, as they still were a family. She sat a moment in silence and then the tears just poured down her cheeks. Dale also said to tell her to get rid of that old car before she had to walk home in the cold one night from work. Lorie began to laugh, as she had a 20-year-old car that was on its last legs and she was holding out to get a credit card paid off, but she knew it was not going to last that long.

She had wanted this very special kind of moment to happen for months and it was just amazing that she had gotten her wish granted in such a special way, from a total stranger, who was utilizing clairaudient ability, in a bar at an airport, where she was not even supposed to be right then! I explained to her God has a way to get messages to us and we all have the ability to communicate with the departed, that with practice we all can converse with our loved ones. If you sense their presence, just acknowledge it; they love to know you can hear or feel them. Time can make a visit very possible for any of us when we believe.

Our time was up, as my flight was ready to board. When I left, Lorie gave me a big hug and asked for my number, feeling she would need my help again in the future. Sometimes it is good to share a moment of caring for another. As Peter always says, heart to hand.

* * * * *

The sense of hearing is one that brings you the opportunity to communicate with others and grow for the betterment of your soul and those you are involved with. It offers a safety mechanism to be cautious about what may lie ahead for you and assist those who are calling for help. It also can be used to gain knowledge and make decisions accordingly.

Be it understood, the life work of each soul can still progress if the physical hearing is taken away. Vibrations through the sense of touch can help the body correct for safety and compensate for any hearing loss. The Spiritual Sense of hearing can be used with the soul's spiritual growth and one's need to use this shall draw the assistance of non-physical helpers and beings of light. The capacity to gain knowledge from another time and space offering protection is paramount.

Spiritual Sense hearing is a commanding sense that offers compassion and love to all who call your Earth home and should always be used in a positive way. Unseen guides will provide you with inward messages through your spiritual ears that you may use for your safety and growth. Many gifted humans are able to use this sense for communication with those living in the afterlife, offering comfort to others for the loss of their loved ones and the guiding messages each soul can experience if desired. At the time of loss of the physical sense of hearing, those who are maturing on the spiritual path shall develop their spiritual body sense of listening and their hearts shall open for a new way of life to receive guidance.

Smell and Taste

I have a lot of calls that reference the sense of smell and the sense of taste, and always wondered how this spirit connection could be so active with people who have not experienced the spiritual body senses. I have had the opportunity to experience these two senses from my own family members who have passed and I know they do exist from my own personal foundation of experiences. I'm going to give you two readings here that reveal different incidences that I have shared with clients and they with me.

This first one was a couple, Stephanie and Brent, whose home required a spiritual cleansing, because they started experiencing some strange happenings after they moved in. I had talked with them on the phone a few days before my arrival and they were having arguments out by the pool area, thinking they felt a presence that just would not go away. They didn't sense it was a mean or evil presence, but one that made them feel guilty for being in the house. So needless to say, I had a spiritual cleansing appointment to hopefully help some spirits find a new home!

When I arrived at the house and got out of my car, I was walking the path to the house and noticed a strong smell that was very familiar to me, as I previously had been a sales representative for Revlon in my youthful days and I sold Charlie Perfume! I rang the doorbell and as Stephanie opened the door to greet me, I blurted out "Who at your house is in love with the Charlie perfume by Revlon?" She looked at me like I was a nut case and then she laughed hysterically saying "It was my mom, Donna! She wore it all of the time. She adored it. Almost too much for all of the family," continuing to laugh.

I asked her to walk outside with me for a minute where I approached the fire pit and asked what was buried under it. She stood there for a minute then started to cry; it had Donna's ashes under it. They had temporarily buried her there because she loved the outdoors of the Arizona desert at night; she used to sit out and have a glass of wine or two looking at the beautiful evening stars. They just felt it was the best spot for her, as she was planning to move to Arizona to be close to them before she passed away that same year. It seemed a good place to hold her ashes while they were deciding a place to spread them to set her free, the way she always wanted to be in the desert – free.

Another connection Donna was making with them was the smell of steaks grilling in the house when there were no steaks even in the house. Her mom loved cooking out and they would always sit outside and enjoy the evenings. Well, I did the cleansing for them, but it was really just to clean out the previous owner's energy and I did a blessing for the new home for mom, as she was definitely grounded and there to stay. No longer did the family feel guilty in their new home; they felt pretty special that Donna was warming the outdoors every night for them to enjoy the beautiful view of the Arizona skies right by her side.

This next reading was an interesting experience for me as well as for my client, Paula, the mother of two young girls about the age of four and another in grade school. The girls had lived in their maternal grandmother's childhood home since birth. The grandmother, Bertha, stayed with them in the winters and with her other daughter, Paul's sister, in the Georgia Mountains for the summers.

During the time the girls were getting into the "terrible twos," their mom, Paula, laughed about how they would talk a few times a week about Poppy, their friend who was smoking in their bedroom while they would have tea parties and it smelled really bad. One afternoon the next year when Grandma Bertha came for her winter stay, Paula was telling her about the girls having a friend called Poppy who usually came to smoke at their tea parties, and lately was also hanging around when they were going to bed. He had become a big part of their bedtime rituals, as they would smell his smoking.

Bertha reminded Paula that her dad's nickname was Poppy, that he was a heavy smoker, and that the girl's room had been his smoking room! As Paula marveled that she had forgotten those details, Bertha was getting more and more distraught because her husband had died in that room and she was frightened that the girls were having some kind of contact with him or someone else may be hanging around them.

I was called pretty quickly when the story began to unfold, as the older daughter had also smelled smoke once in the house, too, but forgot to mention it. We made an appointment for a time that I could meet with the family; I knew this appointment was going to be a wonderful experience for me and hopefully the family, also.

As I pulled into the driveway, I noticed in the window of a parked car an "In Memory Of" decal which some family members place in honor of someone that has passed, usually the car of the deceased which stays with the family. Before I met with Paula's daughters, I sat down and asked about the decal in the car window and learned Paula's husband had passed just a few months after the girls were born. I asked if she felt his presence around at all and she had not. I could tell Bertha was getting upset as we continued to talk about the dead and the family's experiences. It was now or never to calm the grandmother's concerns about the possibilities of connecting with the deceased. I asked if she had ever had any experiences with maybe being contacted by someone who had passed and amazingly she had!

When her husband Poppy had passed, she decided to take off his wedding band and wear it around her neck, as it was the only piece of jewelry he had owned. She wore the ring for years and one day the chain broke. She put the broken chain and ring in her purse to take it to the jeweler the next day and immediately forgot about it. A few weeks later, she was changing her purse and remembered the ring was in the purse but she couldn't find it. It was gone! She was so upset and looked for days to no avail. Time passed by and eight months later she was telling a friend about her loss and that night she said out loud that she sure wished she knew where the ring had gone and she hoped Poppy was not upset with her for losing it. Her birthday was two days later and the ring was literally on her night stand sitting on a small mother-of-pearl box that had been there for months. The ring had not been there earlier, as she had placed her earrings in the box before going to bed. She sat down and thanked her husband, knowing he had somehow put his ring on the box. What a birthday present!

Paula was surprised that her mother had never told her of the story. The grandmother said she was afraid she would not be believed and kept it a secret. After that, she felt Poppy around a few times and that was it; he just seemed to know she was okay then.

I have to say, the only thing I needed to do was tell the Paula and Bertha that those little girls were going to be just fine. They had a wonderful connection with their Poppy and probably would all get to know their dad in the same way as they got older. The oldest daughter and I had a little talk and she did feel she had been contacted by her dad the night he died. She said she heard his voice telling her to be good and he would see her again soon. It seemed like the whole family was having their own little had added stockings for Poppy and the kid's dad on the mantle. The girls were freely talking about their Poppy and, upon seeing pictures of their dad thought they had seen him before, too. They still were pretty young, so Paula and Bertha will know someday just how much the girls are learning beyond being able to smell grandpa's smoke, guaranteed to have a gift for the taking and a blessing for the keeping.

* * * * *

The sense of smell is a tool that can be used for protection and comfort of the body and soul. Danger can animate smell and alert man to get away from it, such as in the wild hunting for food or eating something that may be contaminated, and even to seek protection from weather or harmful toxins baiting the body as food. It can be said that smell is very connected to the heart, as you are able to sense the odor of another's being compatible for love, companionship, and safety. It may also allow humans awareness of the sexual desires of another. The heart shall brim with love from the fragrance of flowers, and experiencing nature through smell allows the mind to sync with the body for greater health.

Smell can sometimes be lost over the life of the human through age or health issues and be compensated by the spiritual body's sense of smell when asking for assistance from non-physical helpers. To have this spiritual body sense of smell can be a great benefit for man, as when danger shall be around him he will be able to connect with this innate ability instantaneously. It should be said again, the ability to receive assistance from beautiful, non-physical beings is strictly through your request.

This sense has helped many people become aware of non-physical beings, including loved ones who have departed and want to connect. One may sense the odor of smoke as well as perfume; these are calling cards from a friend or family member for you to find comfort in this porting ability of the loved being. This experience can be quite helpful for those having begun their transition to the afterlife. The loving connection shall help them know they have just made a heavenly visit.

Much like odor, the spiritual body sense of taste can also be found in heavenly connection with departed ones, as spirits may use that to help man remember friends and family in the afterlife. The Spiritual Sense of taste can help those of you who are becoming aware of your senses; taste can alert you to your other body's senses and increase them to assist you in a time of need for the soul's protection or for information that is required. The sense of taste offers the human knowledge about any health issues the body may emit through this channel.

There will come a day when the senses will all be understood as avenues of communication for the purpose of dialogue. It is of great honor for every human to use these; make every effort to call them your highest gifts from God. Always enjoy them with only the best of intentions for all who reside in the universe. They shall grow as you practice and trust that they are there for the opportunity of the work needed at this time. Heart to hand has now come full circle if you shall honor the beautiful senses God has blessed you with.

Spiritual Senses

When Peter and his friends completed Spiritual Senses for this book, I decided not to add a psychic reading, but instead talk a little about my beginnings with developing my gifts and the process I go through when I do readings for my clients. There are so many times I have been amazed by the accuracy of my readings; I absolutely know am blessed to be in this position of providing guidance. Hopefully, I can give you some insight to a psychic's work.

When I was a child of about five, I noticed colors in the air and around people. When they were happy, the color would be pink; if they were angry, the color would be red; and if they were angry or not being nice at the moment, the color would be dark. Very young, I just figured it was a normal thing to see colors and when someone was going to get angry, I "made for the hills," so to speak. As a child growing up in the South with a father who would be mortified if I started talking about these strange happenings, I quickly learned over time to keep my skills to myself. It would have been a very difficult situation for the neighbors to have that information, as it was considered the work of the devil.

So the one thing I was very aware of was not to discuss the information I received with passers-by, as I understood it was not my place to share, even though I knew it certainly was coming from Spirit – just that sharing not part of my gift then. Over the years, I used my gifts occasionally when I felt it was safe to speak and help someone. It took some time for me to understand colors, how they relate to our emotions, and how I fit into the picture with this knowledge. Colors now are a big part of my skill set and can be used for many events or readings. If you are looking to practice your ability of sight, I would recommend this as part of your homework. You will find it very useful in your future abilities.

It is also a good time to tell you that "Use it or lose it" has a good bit of truth, although it is like riding a bike. You'll pick it up again, but it may take a while to get yourself back up to speed. Always start with meditation and sit in stillness on a daily basis. Actually, it just may come back with some new skills. Meet them with open arms no matter how hard they appear to be. Believe me, it will be worth the work.

Over time I would do a few readings here and there, but still under cover, and I started playing games with myself to see how far I could get with the skills that had become such a big part of my life. Every day I would receive some kind of message that would give me the encouragement to look for answers. This gift has granted me the courage to step outside of the box somewhat over the years, thus helping me leave a successful, sales career and start a business called Feng Shui Concepts, which is still in operation to this day. And that business provided me with huge divine intervention that changed my life forever, literally placing the right people in my life who nudged me along the way to do professional readings full-time. By this time, I was having spirits coming to me and able to talk with those who have passed, in turn giving their loved ones validation of their having made their transition smoothly.

The process for these connections with Spirit come directly from voices and visions that come in — there are no two connections I receive exactly alike. Sometimes when spirits are communicating, they may show me a special ring or watch, sometimes a particular house they lived in. Many clients just want to know these spirits are okay and receive validation they are really there talking with them at the time. There are some things that come in that the client finds funny so it gives them relief and helps them *find peace knowing they have made a true connection with their loved one.*

I have worked on missing-persons cases where I have received information that comes directly from the person's spirit; that kind of information can come flooding in with very distinct clues as to locations that are thousands of miles away in another country, which have been absolutely correct and all of it just comes directly through my speech with no voice or visions. When I have received confirmation of those details, I am floored that I have been completely correct; it is a feeling like none other.

This is a good time to say, just trust in what you get from the universe; non-physicals will be helping you more than ever before. Understand that if you doubt your skills, you shut them down and end up back at square one. It can take a lot out of you and be very distracting. Always give a "thank you;" that goes a long way with them. In addition to the instant "thank you" for their help at the moment of contact, I make a point to end my night with a special prayer for all of my psychic helpers and my guide, Peter, for all of the help I have been blessed with during the day. Being grateful for this wonderful gift is a good thing to repeat as many times a day as you are getting help, or just expressing an extra special word of thanks whenever you are feeling it.

There have been readings that are nothing but visions for the entire reading and can be objects that I have to figure out as I go along. Those readings have become very helpful for me, as some objects I visualize are repeated in readings a lot and have very specific meanings. I often have wondered if the readings are directed by a group of spirits who like to play charades. If so, they certainly are good at it!

All the years I have been communicating with the spirit world, I have always made it very clear that none are allowed in my bedroom at night while I sleep. Although I am pretty used to seeing spirits, I just cannot handle the thought of one standing over me while I am sleeping. I might wake up with the shock of my life, so I demand they always follow my rule of off-limits in the bedroom. So one night I had gotten up for water and on the way back to bed, I stepped into my bedroom and immediately stopped and jumped back, as the whole room was full of a gray mist I could literally feel on my arms. This was my first experience of being a tough cookie and I demanded they leave, instantly. The room immediately cleared and I was able to go back to bed. I learned early on, you are in control of your space when you are dealing with gracious spirits only wanting to chat, visit, or just pass through being a little nosy. If they had had something important to tell me, their actions would have been more precise to get my attention.

I am very used to the methods that I receive information through, as they can be just about anything spirits want to use. The thing is, they do have to learn how to contact you and communicate. When spirits first pass over, there is a learning curve for them to make contact. They have to learn how to control their energy level and emit a frequency to assist you in managing your own energy, so you may make that initial connection. Over time you will be able to adjust your level of vibration and be able to hold it to make the contact last more than a second or two.

I think I mentioned that each of us carries a unique vibration and we can be reached by any of our loved ones in the afterlife. Regardless of your location in the world, you can be found. This is very helpful in out-of-body travel, as we all leave our bodies when we sleep. This is a perfect time for a little déjà' vu to take over for you; it will show up sometime and means you just visited another time a little early.

There are times when a spirit will port an object to you for help and that can be very puzzling for the best of psychics. Last year I was going to bed and heard a metal object hit the floor, so I turned on the light and found a Dutch coin lying there. Knowing I did not have any such coins, I sat for a few minutes and waited for a message but none appeared, so off to bed I went. The next night, I was asleep and awoke when I heard another piece of metal hit the floor; again, I got up and there was another Dutch coin, a different denomination. I have since received some information about them and it is an ongoing connection; usually the message will become known to me and what part I play in it. So you see, the psychic world is vast and interesting.

Everyone has some abilities and you can bring your intuition to the forefront and see what your gifts can be. When you are able to master your abilities, you will have wonderful friends to assist you in your life's journey. There are many names for these gifts – clairvoyance, clairaudience, clairsentience, channeling, mediumship, automatic writing, and psychic perception. If you are interested, it would be interesting for you to spend some time researching them; you never know, you could have a gift or two! I am very fortunate to have been blessed with all of these. The one most special to me is automatic writing, and that is the psychic source used to write this book.

Many people are unsure of being able to have a telephone reading with me if they live, say, in Germany or Oregon. I feel you get a reading via the phone that is clear and concise, as I am not visually distracted by your body language and facial expressions while telling you the information that I am receiving. Regardless of your location, I am able to read for you.

With the limited space here, I have only touched the surface of my years working in this field. I do hope you are able to glimpse some of the experiences people like me have and understand a little better the world of psychics and my own reading style.

* * * * *

The Spiritual Senses are known abilities that can be developed by all humans in every world of the universe. They operate much like the body's five senses, utilizing those abilities on a much deeper level. The body's vibration is your gateway to begin this extraordinary path for each human at this time. It shall never be taken lightly nor ignored when the time has come to offer assistance to another human being in their time of need. It shall be understood that no gift of this magnitude called a Spiritual Sense may be used for any purpose other than the betterment of the humans and creatures residing in this universe. When a human reaches the level of the Spiritual Senses, it will be for the purpose of approaching others needing assistance, without personal ego. Should the human ego become involved during any time during this work, know that these skills may falter due to a having created a lower vibration at that time through your actions.

There are many worlds that use only this sort of communication. It is a known method to just think and then the answer occurs in the mind; no words need be spoken. There is a calmness that comes from this energy force that has purity and love within it. There is no temper because communication springs from thoughts of caring and respect. It is the energy of connection that allows the human to pick up the vibration that is used in all Spiritual Senses.

Origin

Know that all humans have the ability to use and grow their spiritual energy with all forms of your known communications. Some beings require a higher level of vibration than others. The body and soul emit a distinct vibration that is unique to only that body and soul, and can be connected with any non-physical entity from the spiritual realm that helps or agrees to communicate when one is asking for assistance. This communication requires patience, attention, and clean, clear vibrations. There is a manner of learning and growing into this powerful way of receiving information from many non-physical entities and they are present to assist you in your journey.

Some are gifted at birth and some have a very long lineage of family who are at some level of Spiritual Sense growth. Humans over the years have tagged this ability "the sixth sense;" we choose for it to be known as Spiritual Sense. It is said all forms of this gift are available to everyone and some use them intertwined as these become known to them. Some experience an accident, such as head trauma or surgery, and come back with this Spiritual Sense consciousness. It is not unusual for these humans to realize they are receiving a special gift to start their lives over. Their gifts can be of many types and develop as the soul absorbs the consciousness forming in their growth.

The injured ones who have near-death experiences feel very strongly what their experience has been and they begin to understand and develop their gift, in their words, as "a way of simplicity." We must say there is no such thing as simplicity with ownership of the Spiritual Senses. We are talking about one's faith in the highest source known to man, your God. The more one practices, the more one shall develop a broader skill and be gifted with greater ability to connect and work with the non-physical entities that have been assigned to that particular soul.

Growth

Never believe you are not gifted in some way as to the spiritual gifts of your God. It is in the DNA of each human and can be activated as we have told you before, but also can be gifted as a carryover from past lives you have experienced. There is always a small portion of your vibration that has this energy in it and can be accessed as once before in your lives and shall operate at the level you shall be comfortable with. The inner knowing of the presence of another is also a spiritual gift of God and this can help you in your time of need, understanding it is just as important as any of the Spiritual Senses. When you feel a presence, acknowledge it and it shall gift you with some response. Try to choose an Earth object to focus on for this connection, to clear the mind and anchor their vibration so you can make this connection on a regular basis. Over time, this exercise will not be necessary, as you will adjust to the vibrations and will make your connections easily and instantaneously.

We would like to ask and assist you to use small amounts of food or drink and not sooner than one or two hours before you choose to practice your Spiritual Sense in stillness, as this shall assist you in being able to raise your vibration to connect with your non-physical guides. Any heavy foods that you eat later than this time shall lower your energy base and cannot assist you in gaining the higher vibration that is necessary for this work. Alcohol, milk, and caffeine should not be used within the same time period. Water is your best source of liquid to keep the body nourished and hydrated. Nuts, fruits, and vegetables are to be considered your staples for body nourishment to keep your energy level high and should be taken on a daily basis for your practice of meditation in stillness.

You will find many humans who are practicing this path for themselves are choosing bodily cleanliness as part of their work. Be it understood, there are times when the body shall have cravings for meats and large amounts of carbohydrates and sweets, but know this practice shall wane as you proceed in your growth to reach your Spiritual Sense. It shall always be said to ask for God to offer you white light to protect and envelop you for your safety and the vibrancy of your experience. It is at this time you may gain additional vibrations that take you into a realm of seeing those you have known who have crossed into the afterlife, if you are ready to receive a message for yourself or another. These are Spiritual Senses that come in the blink of an eye to offer you comfort. Sit in stillness every day with the purpose of being within the light and for any message you receive, you shall have the help needed to understand and use it for the betterment of yourself and the world you reside in.

There are various levels of this magnificent ability to connect to the Spiritual Senses; they may be voices or colors or music that has its own language – a gifted one has the ability to hear and read this great wonder of vibration from non- physical guides, making each note the same as a written word. The mind's eye, or your adaption of the third eye, can grow immensely through meditation and stillness. The Spiritual Senses also include touch, smell, and taste, and all should be used with love of the heart and offer calmness to the mind. The activation of your spiritual gifts shall be dependent upon the desire to elevate your spiritual practice and shall grow based upon the preferred practice.

Assistance

You will always be given the assistance you need from non-physical guides upon your strong request. Operating among others who have similar experiences is always the plan of the universe; remember, "Ask, and the teacher shall appear." The work that your teachers are helping you with is always present to open your mind and help you raise your energy vibration. Asking and receiving shall open communications with those on the other side; this comes when you sit in stillness and listen for the silence, as that is when you will hear the most.

Those with the opportunity to expand this gift are reminded through the mind on a regular basis of the task at hand, not forced into it; they simply know it is there if they decide to undertake this work they have been chosen to do. Many have chosen to stop this gift because of fear and so they shutdown much of this ability. Let it be known, if you are gifted, it shall always be with you if you choose to share and use your abilities with another and decide to grow in knowledge of this extraordinary talent. Each being has a choice to move forward and work with the ones that are assisting them, or put such growth off for a period of time that is necessary for the soul to embrace its desire to move forward and then later perform the tasks needed to perform the work given to them.

There are many who choose to wait years to take on the task of learning to become more aware of their Spiritual Sense, and then the non-physicals assigned to assist them work very hard to help them advance; no one shall be left behind in their choice of development. This can occur at the end of a human's life to assist another in Spiritual Sense growth and is considered their path from the beginning of their contract, to complete this act of connection for another soul's growth just at that time. There is not a timetable for any soul to complete an activated Spiritual Sense.

Remember that any and all spiritual gifts come from higher vibration, which is needed to elevate your life as you know it on your Earth today. There are ways to expand this powerful energy through meditation, stillness, and asking your non-physical guides to help you. Always show thanks for the process as well as asking them for assistance in helping you understand your newfound skill. This offering of thanks we are asking you to use in connection to your Spiritual Sense may seem redundant, but one needs a constant respect for those who offer their assistance in your path at this time. Being in a state of gratitude will also raise your vibration and give you access to higher planes, creating a more pure level of love for those you are helping so they may also vibrate at higher levels.

IMPROVING HABITS

Many habits that man has today could be adjusted, if so desired, by simply scanning the body. Being in the moment gives you awareness. Love is so much the very beginning of your existence, yet it appears to elude so many. Embrace each day with an attitude of love, kindness, and joy, and your life will show change in every way. Being in the present is such a time of need for all who live on Earth with no sense of direction.

To be in communication with the energies surrounding you can help you manifest much in the physical body to promote good mental health and remove fear present at the time. Anger can and must be tempered when it comes to letting go in a rage of damage to other energy fields. Your world cannot become a force of fear and anger when all bring love into its space. Compassion and love should be on the mind of every human on this Earth to change the outcome of the many lives lost in war.

Honor your body and send love and kindness to all breathing entities in the universe. Offering your assistance to others is one way of accepting of God's loving energy for yourself. Messages are all around you and each one is considered

a wondrous gift to each of you; all it takes is simply trusting you are exactly where you need to be at each very moment. Nothing is without purpose in your life, ever.

Love of Self

So many psychic readings came to mind when I read this piece Peter and his non-physical friends chose to write on this topic. The particular reading that I present to you here was extraordinary for me and for my client, Shelley, a life-changing experience. I am honored to have had the opportunity to be part of her evolution and watch her blossom into an extraordinary young woman who has turned her disabilities into a powerful voice and mentorship for children.

Shelley was born into a large family with seven older brothers who gave her much love and support as she grew into a four-year-old, dreaming of becoming an Olympic gymnast. Her brothers lovingly took her to lessons and pushed her to be her best until one day, while playing in the park, she fell off a bar and suffered a spinal injury which placed her in a wheelchair and ended her future career expectations. Unfortunately, her family could not keep her from the depth of her depression and lack of desire to accept her new life. Her oldest brother, Conner, was a client of mine and asked me to do a reading for her as a birthday gift when she turned 21.

When Shelley called for the reading, I could tell her life force was low and her energy was consumed by sitting in the house. She shot down every word of that reading quickly, as there was no desire to work — how could she? She spoke of being tied to a wheelchair and literally had no sense of value in the state she found her body. In her mind, her worth was lost when she had the fall and now her family no longer had a vision for her. They would never see her successful, doing something that would bring her the fame and recognition that her brothers promised for all of the hard work that made them so proud of her before the accident. She had set herself up for a life of pain and was burying the path that Spirit had planned for her.

I asked her to take a look out of the window and tell me what she was feeling. The only words she could manage to come up with were: trapped, worthless, and broken. I told her that her life was getting ready to change in a very big way, but she needed a voice and to breathe energy back into her body. Shelley needed to feel the Earth's love and feel the beauty in every moment of the day, if she would just look for it.

I assured her that her life would change the moment she pushed that wheelchair out the door and started to take in the beauty of what the world had to offer. Everything starts from a seed and she was getting ready to be her own gardener. Her only assignment was to focus on the children playing outdoors at the school across the street. But that meant she had to go outside, roll that wheelchair a short distance, and wait for the bell to send the kids to recess.

Since her breathe was shallow from being only indoors and inactive, she had one of her brothers, Shawn, go with her, making sure she was safe on this short journey. They would stop often and she noted how pretty the flowers were and asked her brother to remind her to gather some when she was ready to head back. She noticed several little ones playing on the jungle gym and it brought back memories of the fun she had experienced on her previous path to becoming a gymnast. Over the next few weeks Shawn noticed how she was excited to see the kids continue to gain strength on the bars and how much more easily she was breathing, gaining her own strength as well, and then being able to go outside on her own.

It had been some time since I had spoken to Shelley and when she phoned again she sounded like a different person, happy and strong. The call for that reading boded more change and blessed a life beyond all dreams she could ever imagine. Seeing the excitement of her watching those kids play, her oldest brother Conner had put together a program and pitched it to the school that would allow her to work with children after school on the jungle gyms for strength training.

Shelley's question to me started with a statement: "I'm going to teach children a beginning class for gymnastics! Could I be successful?" No question, she was on her way to learn self-worth, love, and joy for herself, as well as give love to the Earth she is able to use as her arena for the kids' classroom. Her brothers are excited to see her life take such a complete turn-around and as a bonus to her new skills, Shelley is taking a painting class from one of the high school students. Her passion is learning how to bring the flowers alive on canvas.

* * * * *

Being in the present is such a time of need for all who live on Earth with no sense of direction. This affects not only the body and the mind but also your ability to move forward and create a true path for yourself. White noise outside of the body will always be there and you must train yourself to ignore this negative influence. You are missing so much that has been placed here before you to help your soul's energy thrive.

It would be helpful for you to try a small exercise in your daily ritual using the very breath that goes into the body. The air is floating around you and you're not aware of the Earth's messages in your surroundings each day. If you cannot find truth in what your day has to offer you at any time, it would be best to meditate with long deep breaths. Take in what you know to be good and healthy of the air that is provided and this will help you clear out any impurities you are experiencing. This shall become second nature and will bring you into a more peaceful state to see and feel the Earth's energy and all creatures that are among us.

The flowers and trees that are around you at this time are for all man to enjoy and nurture. It shall be a task for each and every human to respect and emit love to the grass, trees, flowers and bushes making up your landscape. Think as you take a walk on this wonderful land you know as Earth of a way to make it better. Soldiers of Love work through nature to emit energy for all of the breathing entities we call your garden. Honor these great gatekeepers who are helping emotional balance to grow and creating beauty so that all will prosper in this new energy you are generating for yourself and others at this time. It shall always be man's task to be the gardeners of your Earth. Such a gift can only flourish and exceed an expectation of beauty beyond words.

This is also how man should see their own bodies and realize they have an internal beauty that creates outer beauty not just of skin but of a translucent nature. The heart can only expand its energy field from its designated chakra; similarly the other chakras of the body also emit energy and influence how you embrace life and the energies always available to you. This helps you realize how important it is to love yourself – a needed task in your world at this time.

The subject of worthiness for who you are shall come up many times in our words, as it affects staying alive. Remember, the cells need worthiness to grow and maintain their role in managing health for the body.

Love is so much the very beginning of your existence, yet it appears to elude so many. This shall be a remarkable teaching for you in this world moving forward. God will appoint many more in this self-help world that humans are now embracing as the road to travel for getting this energy on a daily basis. It is a must to stay in love every day and give as much of this energy as you receive. This exchange will feed you so much that you will begin to emit appreciation from the pores of your skin, offering it even to mere energy particles passing by and giving this beautiful force of love a chance to grow. This connection among many souls as they encounter each other will further embrace the feeling of goodness in this energy and empower every soul and

Earth creature the opportunity to share it without thought of selfishness.

You need the ability to see how love has more power than any amount of money, precious metal, or any material asset that man covets at this time. Yes, this is very difficult to understand as you have only known a world that has chosen the value of monetary and power achievements over love for so many years.

This is how your world shall grow, having already begun this task at such a rapid pace. You will see changes happening in very small ways and watch as they grow into large pods and move into businesses as well as men's hearts. It is the job of this energy to change the world one person at a time until it reaches the top of the corporate world and gets the job done to shift Earth for the better without selfish deeds. That is what needs to be done.

It seems like such a long path up the mountain but it is only one small step at a time, each a budding rose on solid ground. We will talk of this many times as we move forward in the future. Man is the tiny pebble dropped into a pond, making such a profound movement, and through your mind and hand it shall grow to cover the whole pond and all of this Earth one day soon. Small gestures performed by each of you will allow you to see the new jobs coming to promote spiritual growth that are already beginning to line up in your space. This is how you will receive validation of strength and purpose from the Soldiers of Love for all of Earth's humans and creatures to achieve the highest level of pure love for your world to survive and thrive.

This is God's desire for man to choose through his own free will and start moving forward the massive pods of love created by small gestures, realizing that free will is God's gift for man to finally use for good and reap the rewards that have been a long time coming for Earth. Every living thing that emits and needs energy to survive and grow in magnificent ways will find this is heaven on its way. There is much for all humans to ponder on this subject. If you should have questions we will give you the answers, as we have nothing to hide. We are teachers of our Lord. We are not the deliverers of times and dates, just messengers of hope and education for a better voice that man can change the ways that have proven not to work.

Attitude

I am so moved by this writing, as it shows the absolute love that radiates from this beautiful group of angelic helpers known to me as Peter and the non-physical beings who are sharing with you today an unselfish dialog of compassion and affection to fill you up. I remember a client who truly needed love to fill herself up and open the door to walk into a life of joy and peace. There are so many blessed souls looking for the love of their lives, not understanding that releasing anger and pain can bring them to the new start they so desire.

I received a call from Andrea, who was gifting herself a psychic reading for her 50th birthday, so of course I was wishing her a Happy Birthday when she cut me off asking *me to not remind her of arriving at half a century with no man in her life, which she admitted was her biggest dream.*

Andrea had experienced a nasty divorce from her husband Kenny, who had left her for a much younger woman over 20 years ago, and she just couldn't find any man out there who was "decent and not a jerk" like her ex-husband. She also was suffering from high blood pressure and other issues as well as a very high level of anger that she blasted at anyone in her way. She wanted to know if she would ever find love or would she just die alone.

The first words Spirit pushed out of my mouth were about Andrea's anger and the effect it was having on her health and pushing any potential mate out the door. It had a pretty simple statement for her: Look in the mirror and see what you are projecting out to the world; you are exactly what you are loading onto others.

The reading ended asking her to take several steps. First, start making a list of all of her angry outbursts at others and why she made them. After this exercise, turn it around and write an affirmation so she could shift her words into kindness for them and herself. Then place that affirmation on her bathroom mirror and on her computer screen at work. Finally, write another affirmation and place it on the door going into the garage where she would see it every morning, saying she was grateful for the kind words she would remember to say to five people during her day.

Well, that was the beginning of a love affair with herself, and just this small gesture she was performing everyday brought her the man of her dreams. Andrea is now a professional coach, helping others to bring change into their lives. She feels her attitude changed her life and she is teaching the same miracle to others.

* * * * *

Embrace each day with an attitude of love, kindness, and joy, and your life will show change in every way. This you shall find amazing, as even one day passing will get you going on the right path. It is so important to feel the love this planet has for all that choose to make it a good day. How easy is it to change your mind about a glass half-full rather than half empty? This appears to be a very large issue for humans. There are many who will choose to bring this challenge back with them again and again for another session here on Earth. Not all can or want to make this their education. Some feel it is too weak or not important to figure out its best use for themselves and others at this time.

Loving the day and seeing goodness, and all that that brings to you, shall lift you to the highest path in your learning this time around. Many who choose to make the best of life can and will have important jobs on this Earth at this time. This does not say they shall hold a high office, but will censor much of the negative thinking with patterns of kindness that bring smiles to many. They are all around you if you will just interact at this time.

Choose every day to find a person unknown to you to interact with using this process. You shall find many other humans flocking to you in short notice. It shall always be the grace of God to remind each of you to be kind and share in the goodness of gestures and wealth. This does not mean to give away money on the street, but a random act of kindness when money comes to you. You will get it coming back to you by bounties unknown to most people from completing small gestures.

Remember, giving is receiving and your body will let you know this every time you participate in random acts of kindness. As you smile and continue to share many free gestures, you will find yourself more attracted to all who come in contact with you. This is a promise from the universe. Try this for one week, be a giver of gestures and you will get to experience the effect you have started in your new life for your own happiness and that of others. Your chain of goodness will follow you wherever you go. This is a wonderful gift and it will never go unnoticed.

Rituals

Rituals are such a wonderful opportunity to connect with your faith and see the rich circumstances opening up to you when you appreciate the beautiful world we live in. They can come from any thought or action you feel drawn to which bodes an amazing outcome. The reading that comes to mind is about June, a young lady who had graduated from college, completed her master's degree in education, and was setting out for a year of travel through Europe with her roommate, Sasha, before settling into her teaching career.

I remember this reading like it was yesterday, mainly because of June's pure love of life and excitement for the adventures that awaited her and her friend. June called with only one question in mind and that was if she would enjoy her trip and get along with Sasha, as she had not traveled with her before this upcoming trip.

The first thing that came to my mind was distance and what kept appearing was a stop sign with her friend's face on it. This would be a hard one to talk to her about, as she might worry that it meant the trip could be a flop if they had issues. I assured her that I felt this would be more of a compromise they would be able to work out – specifically, Sasha wanting to stay and spend time understanding the culture of each area and June wanting to cover a lot of distance, with so many places she planned to visit.

I asked her to make sure they had copies of passports and ID's and kept their clothes to a manageable carry-on. She laughed as I spoke of how important I felt this was for them; of course, I sounded like one of her parents and that was not what she wanted to hear. The last thing I saw for her was a beautiful church, a good number of nuns and children they would meet, and a large brown coat. She assured me the coat was not going to be hers, as she hated the color brown. Needless to say, I felt she had checked out of the reading after I told her they would be great travelmates and an ugly brown coat was coming into her future.

Just about four months had passed and I had forgotten about the reading until I got a message from June's mother, Kathy, asking if I could call her daughter for a short session. She gave me the number with very little information beyond needing to talk with me. And she did not sound upset, so

I made the call as soon as the time difference worked out for both of us.

June seemed pretty excited to hear from me and quickly began her story of the large brown coat. The trip was great until the women had a - - - mishap of leaving their backpacks at a restaurant table one night while talking to another group and her bag was stolen along with her passport, money, clothes, and jacket. Sasha had spent most of her cash that day and the area they were in did not take credit cards. The lady who owned the restaurant comped their dinner for free, handed her a coat to wear, and gave them directions to a church in the area that could help them find a place to stay for the night until they could get her passport replaced and get money from the bank. She was so excited to tell me the coat was dark brown and it was a little too big, but it was very warm and she was happy to get it!

The passport took two days to be replaced; the church had offered them a room at the orphanage free of charge; and she was able to borrow some clothes until she could buy some in the next town. June was so in awe of the kindness the locals had shown them and enjoyed the children at the church orphanage so much, that making the decision to stay a few extra days was easy – the more so for knowing it would make Sasha happy to slow the trip down and soak up more culture. The nuns were pleased to have them stay for a while longer as the girls in the orphanage were enjoying the new guests, learning some English, and gaining knowledge from the storytelling which was a special treat for them.

When the time came for the two travelers to leave, the children fashioned each of them a bracelet of beads they had made of colored paper and it was such an emotional event for them to say goodbye. On the way out of town, they stopped at the restaurant to return the brown coat but the owner refused to take it back; she wanted her to have it to make sure she stayed warm wherever they were going. June noticed at lunch one day soon after how much she was thinking about the children and the kindness of the nuns as she was touching the beads of her bracelet. Everything felt very different from that day on and she wanted to know if there would be anymore obstacles along the way for them, hence her mother's call to me.

Gladly, I told June I saw nothing to keep them from having a great time during the several more months left on the trip. I hung up the phone knowing there would be changes coming for her when it was over and knew I would hear from her again. Sure enough, the call to make the appointment came through some months later saying she had quite a story to tell. I was getting excited just to hear their adventures, but I also knew something else was coming; it was time to see how it all worked out.

She asked me to take a look at my cell phone, as she had sent me a picture that she wanted to show me. Much to my own amazement, June was standing in front of a small building with children around and had definitely made a big decision – to join the convent, move to Italy in 9 months, and live her life as a nun teaching children at an orphanage.

After leaving the church that auspicious day with her friend to continue their trip, she decided to visit smaller towns and spend some time seeing the schools. She lit a candle in each church they visited just as she had done since they left the convent for their next adventure. Interestingly enough, she also bought some little prayer boxes and placed a prayer in every church she visited until they got home.

June knew her prayers were answered when she told her mother of the decision to become a nun. Kathy had told her she had dreamt of her being in church a few times while she was gone and she could not figure it out until now. The rituals had given June the faith that she would find the right answers to her prayers, which were a new home and the gift of an oversized brown coat.

* * * * *

The value of rituals has been known by man since the beginning of time. Birth is man's first ritual and death at the end of the one's journey on Earth is the last ritual for the soul within its current body. There are human rituals in all cultures of your world, past and present. Creatures and the even the smallest of entities also play out their daily patterns to the energy rhythms flowing, each of their regular movements orchestrated in such harmony with the Earth that it becomes its own ritual for their time on Earth. Rituals can be seen in every moment of time, as people bring faith and energy together into a powerful motion. Their benefit is to produce a wonderful completion of movement, giving the body an opportunity to experience calmness and clarity.

When rituals are used by man, the body reacts to their dynamic action by allowing the brain to reach its peak flow of firing circuits to send the proper flow of energy throughout the body, awakening all cells and triggering optimal performance for all parts of that body. Healing through this practice of compassion and love honors the body at such a time. It shall also be known that the body is in a constant state of healing and rejecting disease, or ailing and accepting disease, literally every instant while on Earth. It shall be the human's responsibility to make a choice each moment for its own path of free will.

When man surrenders to a ritual of love and honor, it shall change the structure of each cell of the body to correctly allow the mind and the body to function at a level of pure trust and acceptance of truth. At that very moment the cells begin to act in harmony, giving you the correct dose of energy and fuel you need to heal and clear the toxins that have become trapped in your body. This shall include any negative thoughts that have been brought in through lack of continuity, which start a small thread of adverse action upon neighboring cells. When continuity is restored, it begins to awaken the body's cells; it shall quickly reverse the mindset of depression and any negativity that has been attached to the body and that breaks down all of the previous work accomplished by the goodness of the soul.

The influence of rituals is powerful in every movement of thought and action taken into the body and mind. You are creating and performing at rapid speed a work of spiritual beauty that each soul is bringing to the Earth at this time. Please make rituals in your life an everyday treatment for whatever shall be at your hand that has been taken out of control with ill-managed thoughts and actions. These rituals will heal your body and prepare you to accept your day with grace and understanding of the work you have to do. It is best to remember that actions of faith move from your loving heart to your helping hand. Having a belief system through faith shall provide you with all that is needed for you to follow your life path with the greatness of recognizing your purpose here on Earth at this time.

It is also recommended for you to measure a time of your day to observe your Earth's rituals. They are called the four seasons, beginning with the spring time of birth, summer time of growth, fall time of perspective, and winter time of death. All are part of the process of your world to help move the human mind and body into new energy that forms with each of these seasons, as all your cells adjust accordingly.

Decide for yourself what you may use as your personal ritual in your waking moments. It may be to scan the body for any pain or emotions coming to the surface at the time. Choosing to follow an awareness of how the body feels shall give your cells the opportunity to start their own ritual of sparking energy to synchronize themselves and create true, loving energy for the new day. This can be a time of meditation for you to ground yourself in joy and gratitude after awakening.

As your day moves forward become aware of how your body is accepting the forces that are surrounding you at this time. Should you receive negative thoughts that would be the time for you to assist the body to align itself in stillness and ask your breath to help purge the toxins that have entered your lungs and are flowing throughout your internal system. In that quiet moment, fill your lungs with white light operating as a pure filter, cleansing as it leaves behind an expansion of much brighter light for the body to breathe and use for speaking positive energetic words of contentment and love as your day continues.

As your bedtime shall come, engage in another ritual of calm review of the day and allow your mind to sift your thoughts for what speaks of peace and wellness for your body as you prepare for your night's rest. This is the time to create gratitude in your meditations for the lessons your day has brought.

Honor your body and send love and kindness to all breathing entities in the universe. Imagine you are sending a personal message for all humans and creatures alike, regardless of their state of condition, good or evil. Extend kindness to assist others so they may have the opportunity to feel this loving energy that is surrounding them at this time. Should they choose to make the effort to receive this pure energy into their body, it shall immerse itself in the loving light of God's powerful presence. Offering your assistance to others is one way of accepting of God's loving energy for yourself.

Fear

Oh, happy days! Every day I receive at least seven or eight calls for a psychic reading about personal relationships. The funny thing is, most all are rooted in fear. One particular reading that comes up is about a very special couple that deserves to be honored in this book. There are also so many soldiers that I would like to honor here; assuredly God knows each of you by name. Your presence and love will always be alive in our hearts every day.

When the call came in, it was the third call in a row about relationship issues and, as I have most likely mentioned before, readings show up in groups for a very specific reason. I was alerted to offer extra special compassion, kindness, and spiritual knowledge in providing the psychic reading for this caller, Carolyn. She was very upset about the breakup she was experiencing with her husband, Gene, who was based in Iraq and not scheduled to return home for five more months. She asked if I could help her understand what was happening and whether there was another woman.

Sometimes I will receive information about a reading that is going to happen that day and this was one of those days. I had just received a vision of an accident coming into his troop's caravan as they were traveling back to their base. I saw no injuries, just a lot of fear remaining from the intensity of the experience. This group of soldiers was on their third tour and very nervous about the next few months, as it was to be the last tour for all of them. They were aware of the times that soldiers in their last week or so were killed before they could return home. I assured Carolyn she was the only one in her Gene's life and likely would be patching up this relationship if she could overcome the anger that was causing the issues they were experiencing in the relationship.

Gene's career as a captain had been very dangerous and some of his troops had suffered major injuries with loss of limbs and a death. As much as he tried to give comfort to his wife about being safe, it became very evident this was not working. I saw that the real core of her anger kept going to another soldier in her life and when I asked for the name of the soldier that I kept seeing, it was heart-breaking to find out she had lost both her brother and her dad in this war. I assured her she would not lose Gene but she would have to have confidence in his safe return and release her fear through some faith counseling. Carolyn needed to understand that all of the anger she was experiencing was literally prophesying a negative destiny.

They were able to get past this issue and are happy to report they are still together today and are expecting another child. Gene has since been able to recognize and deal with his own fear and has decided to apply to be stateside for the rest of his service. Carolyn has started a grief group for other mothers and wives on base and has been awarded the use of a small plot there to plant a meditation garden for anyone in need of feeling the energy of their loved ones among the beautiful landscape and flowering trees. They also were allowed to create a walkway for fallen soldiers with words of comfort engraved on the path stones and a wonderful bench engraved with the names and dates of those lost.

* * * * *

The trance state that man finds himself in at times is not by mistake. Sometimes this shall be needed to sync the body with its own evolution, quieting the energies running throughout so it can come to a calmer state needed at such a time. It is at the beginning of the transition through this tranquility that the mind begins to address its words and fears in reverence. This is when the brain begins to bring the neurons to a state of repose that leads to love, happiness and awareness, not necessarily in that order. The body of man is very complex but at the same time is also complete and knowing exactly how to bring each organ, nerve, muscle, and mindful thought to a working stage that can create a new connection among all of the organs, giving the nerves the ability to have a quiet state.

Without this quiet state, man can burn out the nerves in the body and fray them into illness and paralysis. These kinds of conditions occur from fear. We talk a lot about man's fear and how this is a very large part of your experience in the world at this time. As we will show in this writing which will make sense to ones alive today, fear has control over everything that causes negative energy to flow and produces breakdown in the body. Man uses fear daily to control others and maintain his own current status in life. However it stops him from moving forward and realizing his dreams and visions that God is granting each person throughout their life. This is to be known by all and should be studied by physicians and scientists throughout your world; the body has all the answers about man and the direction the world is taking at this time.

When man appears anxious he shoots a spark through the body that can connect with electrical energy in any of the limbs, yet you will see it manifested differently in different people. One is frozen in fear and the legs are paralyzed. Another runs with the legs of an Olympian athlete. Man has great strength at this time or none at all. It is the same way with the brain if you are not charging it; without stimulation you do not get the connection to create dreams, visions or memory of direction, including where you are. There is much to learn about getting the body in sync to be aware of your present surroundings and feelings. It is not such a difficult thing to understand.

Stop when you are aware of fear, take three deep breaths holding your nostrils one side at a time, and continue the three deep breaths. This may make your head ache some, but it is good as you are moving brain cells to stimulate your awareness of the Earth under your feet. Awareness of your surroundings is always of great importance and also the need to speak to the universe; man should feel comfortable talking to the universe on a regular basis. This is very healthy, to be in communication with the energies surrounding you, and can help you manifest much in the physical body to promote good mental health and remove fear present at the time.

Manifesting should not be used for creating fear of any kind, but loving energy for oneself or another human being. Certainly the Earth should always come in man's mind at this time. This is your kingdom; it is of great beauty and you should strive to make it a magnificent place for all to live and work. When your surroundings are clean and beautiful, the Earth empowers itself with good energy. It is part of man's purpose to assist the planet in her growth. Again, be in sync with this Earth; understand it is a breathing entity with a heart and feelings, and that it offers a place to change the energetic direction of fear.

It is understood that your world cannot become a force of fear for all who bring so much love into its space. How you treat this Earth on a daily basis is what you shall reap in years to come, for those who remain in the body and for the souls choosing to return. When the Earth provides you with beautiful flowers, lush grass and trees, and the magnificent blue skies, you must remember it is loving you at its highest level. This also can be felt in all seasons of this great planet and each of those should be honored likewise. There is nothing that God has created for your home without the greatest love for mankind. If these thoughts are always present in your mind, the Earth will give love beyond anything known to man and fear shall not have power.

Anger

Years ago while I was living in Arizona, I would walk very early to avoid the intense heat. My morning meditation included looking above the tile roof tops, seeing the energy floating in a wave pattern that engulfed the perimeter of each house and then disappeared at the edges into the beautiful blue skies. This meant the occupants were living in harmony with their desires and emotions intact. Occasionally there would be homes emitting a dark mist, usually a calling card of angry emotions lingering there. Both types of energy can be taken on by others living in close proximity, just like putting on a suit of clothes.

Many of those latter homes came up for sale on the market pretty quickly after I would see this negative energy. It has no wave motion like the positive counterpart, as it hangs heavily in the air surrounding the house and unfortunately this can bring lasting negative emotion for new owners to assume in their lives without knowing they have taken this influence into their family.

There probably have been a few houses you have been in that held a negative energy in and around it, giving off an oppressive vibe. Many real estate agents call these "unhappy" homes and I prepare them for sale with a spiritual cleansing, actually helping the entire sub-division to welcome the new owners with healthy emotions. Should you be in the market for a new home or having some issues happening where you live, consider getting a spiritual cleansing. You will feel the difference and can create a small ritual for your private space.

Your environment does have a direct effect on your life as well as what you are attracting to yourself as you hold onto negative thoughts. Remember, your thoughts have legs and they can follow you right into a new situation, mirroring back to you what you are trying to get rid of. Peter's material here is an example of the damage anger can bring to humans on a daily basis.

My particular client with regard to this had experienced some definite hardships over the past 10 years of her life and was beginning to have health issues showing up at *the very time she was ready to move on. Faced with a divorce that drained her bank account and losing her job and house in the same year presented her with a mountain of pressure that turned into pure, aggressive anger. High blood pressure was active in her body and her knee issues were to the point that she was facing surgery.*

Lucie's call came in on a cool, fall, Saturday afternoon asking for a quick psychic appointment, as she was sitting with a bag of frozen peas on her knees. The first words from Spirit coming into the reading revealed that her anger was going to increase her blood pressure to dangerous levels and she could lose the ability to get it in control; the knee issue was all about her inability to move forward in her current condition. The words were meant to be a wake-up call for her and she was not taking them kindly. Not many times do I get a client having a little "hissy fit" with the psychic, but I was taking it in stride because she really needed help.

She finally began to talk about taking out her anger on everyone she came in contact with, especially in the car. She was not accepting her part in the road rage events that were becoming a daily occurrence. It was not the big issues that set her off; it was the little things that were building up and the interaction with others who were feeding off of her negative energy.

Spirit asked her to stop and think about the people in the other car she perceived to have cut her off. What could they be experiencing that would cause them to make such dangerous maneuvers with their vehicles? Could they be having an emergency that they need care for, or might they be fired if they show up late one more time at work? Or could they be experiencing the same horrible life issues that you have had? You are not the only one out there with issues; we all have to be good stewards of this world and treat others the way we would like to be treated. (Heard that before?)

I asked Lucie to write in a journal about her rages, when and where she was spewing the negative energy daily and not to look at her writings for two weeks. She was also to journal any of her good deeds such as letting someone go in front of her to take a side road, and notice if they showed appreciation for her kindness. And her biggest assignment was to spend five minutes in stillness before she went out in the morning to think of how it feels to share goodness with others and proceed with that thought all day, even as simply as expressing it through a smile and a wave.

Lucie definitely was going to receive a beautiful divine intervention that would take her down a new path and a life worth living without anger controlling every detail of her day – a promise that would come quickly if she would show some faith and allow the past to be the past. Today would be the beginning of a new life of happiness, joy and, for the first time in 10 years, PEACE.

When she called back a few weeks later, Lucie shared her success about being a more mindful person toward others who were hurrying along in their harried way to get where they were going. When she looked at the journal, she was amazed that the first few days she'd been out of control, spewing negativity to everyone she came in contact with. She then noticed her rages were slowing down and she didn't feel a need to attack others, but to send them good energy with a grin or a gesture. She had big news about getting a wonderful new position, saving money for the first time, and feeling that once she had an understanding how others could be going through a rough patch also, she began to see the need to make changes in her own life.

She calls for check-ups pretty much every month, her knees are not painful any longer, and the doctor shared the good news that her blood pressure issues were making big strides in getting better for her age. No question, Lucie has made great improvements in her life and hopefully many others will also experience the mirror effect of love and patience.

* * * * *

This day brings much to say about anger, an emotion which can change the body in ways that are damaging to the cells and the blood vessels that underlie the type of life you have here on Earth. Anger can and must be tempered when it comes to letting go in a rage of damage to other energy fields. It is not necessary to cross over into a space of rage to handle your emotion at such a time.

The thing about anger or misplaced attitude is that you emit this negativity into the universe and soon as you let it go out of your body, either by word or action, you are poisoning the energy that is collected by others in the air that everyone breathes. Then it shall be brought into the body and become each person's own until they release it or send it to another soul. Your job here is not to project your negative energy on man or creature. That energy is alive and can attach to anything that comes into its space.

Some encounters that man can create without direct knowledge of this negative energy are called road rage. Such interaction between two souls can become violent and neither realizes their part in affecting the environment. Every morning before you leave your home it would be nice to include the following ritual for your safety. Stop and remove your shoes and feel the solid surface below your feet. Take a breath from your toes all the way to your lungs, raising your hands to the heavens and imagine what a great being you are and why you are alive today, being blessed with breath at this time. Blowout this breath, feel the release of any negative thoughts you may have at this time and instantly eliminate those thoughts from your brain. This shall mute how the energy you hold within your body becomes toxic to your Earth.

As you leave your house each day and commute to work, be mindful of your thoughts and how powerful you are. This small gesture can help change those around you and the chain reaction you create can begin to shift the world. You have that power! Send loving thoughts out into the world to pass on and if another being's energy field needs positivity then it shall connect with them. A smile goes a long way, even to yourself. This we shall say many times to you in this writing.

Remember also to stand tall and feel the energy flowing through each of those blood vessels we have just talked about. This will become a mindful way of life if you practice it on a regular basis. How long is regular, you say?

The answer is as often as you are reminded to do so. Listen to your own thoughts; this shall be the thermometer to tell how much is right for you to do. It shall multiply for you and then it will become part of your daily routine.

Many habits that man has today could be adjusted if so desired by simply scanning the body. By this we mean feel the muscles and the tensions you are experiencing. They tell you if you are holding your body in such a way to cause pain in any area. If your habit is looking down, leaning over as you walk, and then you have a backache; you are receiving information from the body that it is carrying too much on your shoulders and you need to release this energy now. Standing erect allows the blood to flow correctly and clears many issues in your organs. If you dread your way to work, change it up. Walk around the building, feel the air on your cheeks, and look at the majestic trees that are living beings working on your behalf, helping to change the energy you currently are carrying. They are powerful sources to cleanse the Earth of negative energy.

There are so many messages that are available for you to receive from just a simple walk outdoors. Look up to see the brilliant blue sky and watch the clouds float by, forming different shapes of babies, animals, angels, balls, fish and so many more things. Be in the moment; look and as you see a cloud taking shape, notice it is forming precisely for you. There are many angels working the sky waiting for your awareness of this simple beauty you are experiencing in the moment, allowing your body to feel the connection to God just by viewing this gift of the sky that He shares with the masses.

Being in the moment gives you an awareness of something as simple as a broken twig lying on the ground before you. Just to experience it being there can help you understand that the broken twig is going to be replaced on the tree it fell from, creating a majestic limb of beautiful leaves that will blow in the wind and across your face. Rebirth is a very powerful experience for man, giving hope and knowledge of what has been and what is yet to come. Pay attention to your thoughts as something catches your eye on your walk, for that may be a good time to pause and realize that a message is forming for you at that very moment. God's messages are all around you and each one is considered a wondrous gift to each of you. All it takes is simply trusting you are exactly where you need to be at each very moment. Nothing is without purpose in your life, ever.

As we have said before, we will alert you to how to receive messages and understand them. Don't doubt any message that comes your way. It may not make sense to you right away; just write it down and in some manner you will come to understand how it belongs to you or someone that needs your assistance in this life. Remember as we go further in this subject, we shall deal with the emotions that confirm the value of your day and time at present.

You are sometimes picking up messages that others have released and no longer own. Sometimes this is good and can benefit others' lives. Many a book, song, or a life-change comes from the appearance of these random messages. You are very lucky to understand them as you grow in your new world of communication. We have more and shall come later in the day.

Wars

When I think back to the number of psychic readings I have been blessed to provide so many of the brave young men and women of the military, I am in awe of their innate ability to know their purpose and respond without fear or hesitation. It is drilled into each of them to never lose sight of their mission to serve and protect. Many are from very large families that have supported the military for several generations. I am also struck by how each of them opened up to me instantly, offering me their trust and respect for my work. There have been so many times I found myself talking with military clients like old friends. It was as if they had found a confidant who could understand their concerns about moving forward.

When I reviewed this writing, one particular reading came to mind that I had a few years ago with Donald, who suffered PTSD and loss of hearing in one ear. He called to talk about his life out of the service, having a hard time becoming a civilian and holding down a regular job. Since his deployment, he had been repeating the same dream about waking up on a battlefield he did not recognize, before the blast that rendered his current injuries. After returning home as a civilian, Donald began to see a quick picture of another war background where he was a medic helping others caught in the conflict. There was a bold line that was weaving this story with his desire to continue to help others, and upon his final reading with me he went back to school and became a medic in a Veterans hospital.

There have been so many readings that ended helping military people to discover a compassionate, loving path in the civilian world. Many chose to go back to the war areas as civilians to work on bases and offer support with serious injuries regardless of a soldier's medical condition or rank in the service. They became unofficial coaches with an extra ear and heart for someone.

I've noticed they never talk a lot about their bravery and ego was nowhere to be found. But they did say how many times they wanted to lend a compassionate hand to anyone that was hurting, and always felt it was their job to help their brother and sister soldiers. I usually carry a pocket full of quarter-sized angels when I am in the airport and when I see a service man or woman I stop and give them one; I tell them how much I appreciate them and let them know they are also loved.

After reading this I hope you will feel the Soldier of Compassion's humble lot of omniscience, in looking out for these soldiers coming home and helping them find a way that can embrace a life changed forever by their service.

* * * * *

It is the evening to discuss the wars of the world that man is creating at this time. Understand this is not new for this world. It is true there is a raw energy flow and desire of power that infuses this energy into the hearts of souls who have experienced war in other time-lines. Many are here today to complete the process of pain and debate with themselves to never have to come again in any other lives to repeat this work.

Understand this shall not stop in this world's life. This shall be seen as a stage played for those who need to pull power into their own lives at this time. Come and understand all who partake in this world as soldiers, to offer protection for all they leave behind including their country, feeling it is their duty no matter the danger lying ahead.

Many who are signing up for war have spent many lives in this behavior and a desire to protect their countries and loved ones is carried over from previous lives. Some of the soldiers in previous wars who lost arms, legs, and suffered severe head injuries have come into another war losing the same body parts and suffering the same injuries. This is being done to try and complete the past-life fear and anger that came with such injuries from war times.

The soldiers coming home today from your current wars are determined to heal their injuries and mental emotions and try to lead a normal life. Some of these soldiers have had premonitions, déjà vus of what was to come before they were injured. This has been a bleed-over from a past life in one's memory of past wars. It is up to the soldier to emotionally complete this call of duty.

These injured soldiers are met by the Angels of Mercy at their hospital door. These angels remain beside them daily and help in every way possible to heal and put the words in their reach to begin the healing they need. They emit the beautiful energy of compassion to help soldiers cope and decide right then if they choose to live out their free will. Others carry over the work into another lifetime to repeat this job they have chosen many times over. It is not a choice of God to cripple man or woman nor take their lives in these wars. This is the decision of the soldier to come forward on his own and use his free will. As we said earlier, many realize life shall be short on some level and many also understand the seriousness of using their free will to direct and be directed into harm's way.

Shall one who needs to complete the lesson of protection go home to his own karma and have no need to fight another war? The guilt that many feel is an emotion that moves them to understand the need to feel energy for others at this time. It is not their desire to feel anything negative and many turn their hearts to connect with God for forgiveness for any lives they have taken. Many feel all will be well for those they had protected. The soldiers do not look at their bravery at this time, but more at their need to love and receive the same for their broken lives.

All who are not fighting these wars should send the joy of love to these brave souls. They can help in a very big way with a little gesture on their part. Create a small part of your daily ritual to pray for these souls and spend time with a vision that shows all returning home safely.

When there is talk of war, the human mind begins to process the negative and permits it to grow into an extraordinary amount of anger and a desire to move ahead without much thought of the outcome. Instead, come and feel what this energy can begin to do if these thoughts are reversed with love, and how it can lead all men to greater compassion. It is left up to people with free will to assist all humans in this state of mind. Compassion and love should be on the mind of every human on this Earth to change the outcome of the many lives lost in war. Being mindful every day of this disease called war can end with the removal of ego and personal power men choose to use against each other.

TENDING EARTH

We speak of loving kindness and compassionate grace, and many consider them words for the New Age. Not to be, we say; they are words for now. The Earth is loudly calling for human desire to save this world and to move toward a restoration of helping all who currently reside here. The human body is losing alignment with the purpose of its structure, suffering from the use of chemicals because of what man calls "convenience." Negative discussions are operating at a very high level in the direction of the unhealthy energy that is not good for man. Much has to do with the mindless focus on illusions of beauty that are not attainable.

If time were spent watching the wonder of God's species, you would find they also have also obstacles finding food and doing what it takes to obtain it. Living in the moment is how the animal kingdom chooses to survive and without this beautiful instinct, not much would be in existence at this time. Man can live a much calmer life by choosing the animal approach in choices they make each morning and not allowing negative energy to start their minds and lead the day as it goes forward.

There are opportunities for everyone to ensure the world's energy is rising to a level of love for all that man has. Take a look around and speak of gratitude for the beauty of this world; notice how flowers are not the same, each very unique from other even as they are all equally beautiful. Create a loving environment for all; that is what man is here to do. There has been a time chosen for this action and it is now upon you.

Realistic Expectations

This reading came to me several years ago and it still feels just as powerful now as it did then. I usually don't answer the phone that I use for readings after seven p.m. unless the appointment has been set up in advance. The reason is that I do psychic readings for people from all over the world and if I'm not careful, they will go well past midnight and into the very early morning hours. Having this time limit works for me and I have pretty much settled into that way of life for many years. So when the phone rang late one evening, I decided to pick it up out of the ordinary because I had a feeling it might be particularly important. Well, it proved to be just that.

The lady said her name was Mary Anne and asked if I could do a reading for her right then. I hesitated for a moment and something just said "Do it." I could feel her energy as really down, somewhat depressed. I asked if she had had an accident, as I saw a hospital bed with a calendar that showed eight months in a row, and right beside the bed there was a fire and someone struggling to put out. I asked if that made sense and she replied yes, but the number of months was only partially right, as she had spent 2 additional months in another hospital on the West Coast for plastic surgery.

When she said she wanted to know if she would ever be pretty again, I knew that fit with the picture of the fire. I asked how bad her burns were and her reply was "Any burns are bad." Mary Anne had lost everything to a fire from a cigarette left unattended as she was taking a nap in her living room. She certainly was fixated on her disfigurement, talking about scars on her hands, the right side of her neck, and chest.

She spoke of having been a young model for a local department store with plans to go to New York for a modeling job at a small company that had connections with her store. Mary Anne knew she had the right figure and face, and wanted to be one of "the beautiful people," because they were always sought after and she knew that money and men would pour in with the gift of her looks from God. Then a month before her trip, the accident happened.

The tragic fire took away her big dream; she would never be pretty again and never work in the modeling field that she had worked so hard to be a part of. Her friends went on to become successful in the fashion business and were living "the good life," and here she was struggling just to get healthy again. She felt her whole life had stopped and she never went anywhere except to see doctors. Mary Anne had truly put herself in a situation from which it was unlikely to create the artificial beauty that was so important to her.

She seemed to become angry when I talked of what constituted outward beauty and how her inner beauty was beginning to shine through. She said she had spent so much time and money getting the right plastic surgeons to tweak a few features because she had felt was important to be prettier and get rid of all the flaws she saw in herself. Mary Anne believed she didn't need whatever I was talking about, especially inside where she felt no one could see her.

There was no doubt this young lady still had a beautiful presence inside and out, and had made great progress in healing her scars. There was definitely a career in the beauty industry for her; she just had to believe it and choose to make the small adjustments in her life to bring it to fruition. That was going to be her most difficult transition, but not impossible.

The last few minutes of the reading I asked her to make a list of each component she found interesting in the world of modeling and fashion, and write a letter to herself about what it felt like to help another person with less experience in the business that she dreamed being part of, and to be honest about what she felt her real beauty was. We made another appointment for three weeks later when we would cover the material that she was to complete. The last words I gave to Mary Anne were how grateful I was to have picked up the phone that night. I made it clear that I expected her to use the same words for herself about anything she wanted to announce her gratefulness for to the universe as many times a day as she could.

The call came in for her next reading and I felt a shift in her that was positive and even kind of enthusiastic. She explained that creating the list of things she liked about fashion and modeling was a bit of a work but she had done it. There were so many components to the whole modeling job that excited her and she was making some contacts with her agent to see what the odds would be for her to find a job that didn't require her to be in front of the camera. Mary Anne's next words were how grateful she was that she had written the list and that she really felt the energy of it. She saw for the first time that beauty does not come from a person's appearance, but the inner beauty that is conveyed when you are being true to yourself – she realized that she was finally getting it!

It seemed difficult to believe she had any opportunities that did not require her to focus only on her beauty, but she was going on a mission to find that job and make it a lasting career, scars and all. Her inner beauty was coming out very nicely, I must say. Her scars started fading and allowed her outward beauty to move back to the forefront, just as predicted. Mary Anne knew she would find her place in fashion and understood the gift of gratefulness.

Just about a month later, she called my office for another reading and when that call came in, I was so happy to hear the excitement in her voice as she told me she was managing commercial shootings all over the West Coast, in charge of models' contracts and acting as their producer. She had found her new home in the fashion world and was off and running, looking for more locations for her models. She spoke of her ability to help them when they were feeling *down and not in sync with their bodies, that she was always available for words of encouragement. Mary Anne had known kindness was in her, she just needed to grow and share it, and that she does every day now with new models and their dreams.*

* * * * *

This night shall bring much to say about the health of the world you know today. There are many ways to look at mankind during this time. The humans living on Earth all have energies not fitted for them at this time. Much has to do with the mindless focus on things not related to their lives; the focus of this world is based on illusions of beauty that are not attainable at any time. The exterior of the body is only to give the soul a home, to contain and protect all of the organs and the inner workings needed for complete functioning. Every human is unique in looks, size, color and any other traits including deformities of the body. There is beauty absolutely in every human being that makes their home here on Earth.

The beauty of each human has to do with the soul and the heart's core. You are in many ways having issues with staying in the state of mind for man to focus on their own truth and well-being. Much can be said about feeling you need to meet the standards of neighbors, family, and peers. What can you bring to the real health and work of this Earth for the soul? It is not competition. You are not here to compete, but to complete the missions of the soul's life. This shall include your teachings of living a better life and healing the Earth, which has been given much abuse over time at the hand of man.

There is some small glimmer of hope for this change in the coming few years as you are trying to create a green world. This is man's definition of cleaning and being given a chance to not be so hard on what God has gifted you in this world you call home. Many of the creatures that also called Earth home have disappeared over time as your history has shown you, but many will be coming back in other forms. These creatures also repeat their past lives in other bodies. Man has not even scratched the surface of what is living in some of the space and time of this world in which you currently reside.

Man should take a softer approach to sharing Earth and will do so soon with help from Soldiers of Kindness. Yes, they do exist, and cover everything from cleaning up your waste to bestowing kindness to all creatures. One of the glorious attributes for this beautiful entity will be to create a large pod of kindness elevating the warmth of the body, connecting the heart with the head. This is the sensation that you will feel when you help your fellow man in some way. This kindness shall be a realization of the need to be of assistance to others in any ways possible.

This seems to become prevalent around your holidays, when the heart is festive and giving is such an easy, good feeling for you. Our purpose is to help you get to the place of every day feeling the need and desire to consider kindness for all mankind, including the worlds' creatures. We are seeing this working in small gestures now. If you will share some small gesture every day, you will be the beneficiary of this love and will understand the purpose and the value of the Soldiers through the coming months and years.

This can change your world in magnificent ways including your health and your Earth's vibration. You will live a richer life and love will permeate through you and touch all who surround you. Your workplace will also improve. Love is very contagious, like negativity can be, and you will have the opportunity to experience the value of love. You will never want to go back to the negative.

Heal Your Earth

Wow, if each of us dedicated five minutes every day to help this Earth regain its health and beauty, it could provide enough energy to emit the pure love to heal many of the illnesses we are dealing with today. There is always a beginning point and it does not have to be a huge project – just start in our small communities and let the universe assist, as the non-physicals around us are more than willing to support the requests in our hearts.

This brings me to a special reading from a young couple, Patty and Derrick, who both grew up on farms and wanted to continue that lifestyle, but due to financial constraints they ended up living in a historic, multi-level apartment in a large city working off their college loans. I received the call from Derrick, who had a major concern for their health, as their animals and young son were experiencing some health problems. They were concerned enough to contact the state's environmental department and sure enough, there were conditions in the building which proved to be unhealthy for occupancy. The more he looked into the surrounding area, the worse he found it, and made the decision to look for a location elsewhere. His question was where, what, and how could they make this move with little money and working with the school systems; he felt he was limited.

Well, Derrick was amazed when I gave him the specific name of a small community to check out in the western U.S. and verbally outlined a strategy to find a teaching position that could provide the money needed to live and pay the student loans off. I gave him some other alternative words from Spirit and we agreed to talk again as they were ready to put the plan into action.

Nine months later, I received a call from Patty and she had some real interesting news to share with me. They had followed my advice and found a community not far from the original location we'd spoken about. Looking for a small home, they found an old farm that was badly in need of work with an option-to-buy after one year of renting. To hold down the cost of living, they planted a large garden and noticed the neighbors began asking how to grow the vegetables and plants they wanted to use in alternative healing modalities. They came upon another young couple in the area, an acupuncturist and a holistic doctor, both interested in partnering with them to start a healing facility for students to come and learn alternative lifestyles with diet and holistic practices. As part of this therapy and education with meditation, massage, and nutrition, they created a small retreat for people to come and help on the farm.

Their success was just amazing and the shrinking community began to thrive again as many small businesses sprang up to expand the mindset of taking care of the Earth, learning how to live from her bounty, and honoring her for providing the master love she has to give to all humans who are here on this planet today. By the way, the college loans have been paid off in full and their faith is very much intact for the blessings they are able to enjoy and share beyond their community. Others are choosing this lifestyle from the simple desire of one small family wanting a healthier environment and the opportunity to give back to the gracious world we share.

* * * * *

This evening shall bring a new topic that should be on the minds of all humans at this time; the information that follows will be of assistance to everyone. The human body is losing alignment with the purpose of its structure, suffering from the use of chemicals that are settling into the cells at this time. This is occurring because of what man calls "convenience," wanting to remove the work from cleaning and daily chores. There has been much happening on this Earth that drains it of its own natural resources of clean water and air. All humans, creatures, and plant life need the Earth's ability to produce pure air and water to keep this world growing.

The body is in great need of the same flow of clean fuel as a flower or a tree. Breath is the basic function of all living entities in your world and is at the root of the diseases man is suffering in real time today. For the body to function it needs to have movement of growth in its cells; otherwise the impurities get lodged, blocking the healthy delivery of oxygen to all organs. The brain functions at a low level at such a time and the cells begin to return unclean matter, causing it to shrink and not achieve the correct electrical charge to pulsate within all the other organs. This weak pace needs to change in order to create a clear path for the oxygen and blood functions at this time.

The Earth is now loudly calling for human desire to save this world and to move toward a restoration of helping all who currently reside here. There is much happening to change the course of destruction at the hands of the "convenience" that man has created today. As we have said many times, it is your free will to live the life of your desire; we will never interfere with your decisions. Nevertheless, we must tell you the toxins that have appeared in this time continue to grow at rapid speed and not only alter the Earth's ability to breathe but also the ability of man to do the same. It is important to bring man's desire to re-create health and all shall benefit greatly. It shall always be our desire, for the love of all humans, creatures, and plant life, to assist you to live a pure life for the proper time you have here.

There is a movement that has begun for accountability in saving your Earth, begun by old souls who have spent many lifetimes growing this planet to the pristine beauty that is breaking down even as we are speaking to you now.

They will continue to work on many levels for man through careers enabling them the advantage of taking care of their communities. This energy is creating a wave of knowledge to make changes in the body of your families to stand tall and the world is asking for voices that shall grow strong over the next short while.

The universe is opening new pages of knowledge, so that man will raise the cry for reason among all who will listen and allow this movement. This will be seen in the consciousness of each and every human to honor this vast Earth, standing tall against all adversaries who continue a destructive attitude for monetary gain and lack of responsibility. This shall elevate man's compassion and understanding that everything on this Earth has a season of life.

Be it understood, for the life of your world to continue, it is time to speak and choose to move toward the previous state of your world's creation. Come and spend time walking through the gardens of green as they are quickly losing ground to the obvious destruction. It has always been the desire of the universe for man to see this and now it is time to stand up and restore Earth back to its earlier glorious beauty. Upon this time the body of man will make a full transition of health and mindfulness to continue honoring the Earth you currently call home. There has been a time chosen for this action and it is now upon you.

Wonders of the World

A few years ago, I received a call from a woman who wanted to purchase a reading for her old friend, Cassie, who was having some issues. I instantly cut her short so she wouldn't give me information that I felt could affect the outcome of the reading. So when I got the call from this Cassie, it was from my own intuition that I received an instant knowing of her hermit life-style and the helpless feeling of life slipping away from her. After suffering a very difficult divorce and lacking skills to make a living, she was almost at the bottom of the emotional ladder. She had stopped looking for work and just slept most of the time.

We talked about taking baby steps to simply get out of the house and take advantage of the warm, spring days. We talked about how Spirit can send ideas and messages from the universe in gentle ways via nature. Cassie was resisting, but I assured her that when we spoke again she would have some thoughts of her destiny. With some more words from Spirit, I hung up with a promise from her to put her new-found journal to work.

Sure enough, a month later, she called for another reading and had a very different outlook on her future. Cassie spent time out in her garden and noticed she had some new plants growing from some very old organic seeds handed down from her grandmother – seeds which she felt her great-grandmother had started the planting in the early 1900s.

The more she looked around, the more she realized she missed her gardening and decided to label the heirloom plants growing around her. She started visiting some of the gardens nearby and found a quaint nursery and an old man who shared with her his knowledge of organic seeds and gardening. Cassie's internal seed began to sprout at that very moment and helped her grow in the right direction!

On the way home she decided to stop at a used book store to check out information on gardening and she found three books she liked; oddly, the owner didn't even know where they had come from. As they were tattered and seemed worthless for the store, so he handed her the books and told her to enjoy them, no charge. When she got home, Cassie started doing her research and realized the books were written at the turn of the century and she knew right then her job had been created; divine intervention had started long before this trip to this store. Her walk outside to see the beauty of what this world had to share was Spirit's perfect manifestation of an ideal road for a new career and a rapid change in energy and hope.

I have to say, sitting here reading this material once again opens the door showing synchronicity is alive and well. The four-leaf clover they talk about in this material was her lucky charm. Today she is a master gardener and an expert on preserving heirloom seeds which bring many new friends into her life. Cassie gets to spend her time outside seeing what God has to offer, as we all can when we are willing to stop and take time to look around at his creations, take time to smell the roses. I am encouraged by the constant ability to follow a soft voice directing us to take the first step, look around and allow our body's energy to be in sync with God's achievements and the army of creatures who keep things growing.

* * * * *

It is the time of year that you are out and about and there is so much to connect with in your world. Man has been granted so much to observe and search out on this wondrous Earth. Many have the opportunity to travel beyond the homestead they are residing in, while there are also those who have no basis of funds to make any journey. There are opportunities for everyone to ensure the world's energy is rising to a level of love for all that man has. Many go through their daily plans and do not take the time to share joy with others who may very well need this energy at this time.

Wonders of love follow even a butterfly as it shares its beauty and seeds of love for this Earth. Take a look around and speak of gratitude for the beauty of the creatures that support this world, and help the flowers and trees to spread this energy. For all eyes, the flowers are for everything and everyone to harvest beauty.

Show the gratitude of finding a four-leaf clover growing in the ground and ponder the wonder of such a beauty standing out just waiting for you to find it. The special clover is just like man – very unique from other clovers even as they are all equally beautiful and found in healthy in clusters. Like the idea of man getting along with each resident of the community of clovers, they experience great strength and come in all sizes shapes and numbers of leaves.

That is what man is here to do – be part of a community growing strong, realizing we are all unique, but having a close presence with others to be happy. Look around, flowers are not the same. Notice the way they stand; higher flowers helping shade lower flowers just enough so they may grow and come out in the sun. Much like a parent in protecting their little ones, you see humans are to coexist as one with all living entities on this Earth in appreciation of its love and beauty.

So it is man's job to respect the work of God and help keep the world growing, showing how to create a loving environment for all. As you take the trip of your summer, go slowly and remind those around you of the opportunity to show gratitude for all that comes into your space. It is your path that God has shown you, to honor our Lord and one another.

Human Connections to the Animal Kingdom

There is such a beautiful moment early in the morning, sitting outside having your coffee and watching the squirrels quickly running to their special hiding places for their stash of nuts and the birds standing on the side of the nest feeding their new babies. It hit me one day as to how we as humans do live somewhat parallel lives to these wondrous creatures, taking care of our young and working to provide them food and shelter. The awareness for me was so emotional that it brought tears to my eyes thinking about the ones that maybe can't provide this protected life for others and themselves.

So needless to say, I was not surprised to hear from a middle-aged, corporate gentleman named Brian, who was calling for a psychic reading because had concerns about leaving a very profitable career at this stage of his life to start something new. The pull for him to make this change was unsettling since he had already given his notice of retirement and he wanted some advice. He had never experienced a psychic reading before, but I was recommended by a good friend of his and he was so concerned about his urge to leave his career, he felt it may have some merit to help him in some way.

I think I need to clarify my statement about not being surprised about Brian's call. Ever since I was a young girl, I always knew when a certain kind of client was going to call me and as the years have progressed I'm absolutely certain when I've experienced a moment of spiritual knowing. Then I will get a call from a person needing exactly the kind of reading I had just felt from the energy of that knowing. Much to my delight, Spirit had just sent to me the reading of my dreams. As always, I AM grateful.

When the reading began, I could tell my new client was nervous and wasn't connecting to the words Spirit was sharing. However, the minute I spoke about being outdoors and the love of animals, Brian lit up and was totally engaged in relating a dream he had experienced rescuing animals that had been hurt in the wild. Before this reading was over, he had a mindful opportunity for a career and he left with such peace.

Today, Brian has moved to another state to a small rural area with lots of animals and horses. He has become the "go to" man for miles and even states away to rehabilitate all kinds of injured animals. Most of them he returns back into the wild when they are healthy enough. For permanently injured animals, he has built a facility for them to live out their lives safely. This project was also perfect for him and his wife to manifest a place for children with disabilities to help or get involved with one of the new horse programs designed just for children and young adults with emotional issues.

Again, Peter and the non-physical beings show that God gives the right words and emotions to bestow a glorious gift of purpose and partnership, even with the with the animal kingdom, once He is asked.

* * * * *

No morning starts without the soul awakening the shell of the body to come alive with the energy your day will follow. Many on this Earth use their morning ritual of love and appreciation to start each new day in a positive way. They awaken with gratitude, moving forward without letting negativity build into a day of chaos and confusion.

This is a time for all to come awake including God's creatures that have their own rituals. They may clean their eyes and yawn sitting in silence, waiting for the desire to move out of their nests, whatever those may be. Their desire to forage for food is their job of existence, feeding their new family in the spring. The creatures of our Earth have an experience of their new day very much like man, caring and providing for family and so it goes. We are connected very strongly, similar in habit.

If time were spent watching the wonder of God's species, you would find they also have also obstacles finding food and doing what it takes to obtain it. Do they show the same frustrations as man? Yes, in many ways they are like man, but they learn very quickly to pay attention to where the food chain is and if their prey is nearby. They are always listening to their surroundings and they learn when danger is upon them. They understand a need to escape and not return for a potential attack.

Man can live a much calmer life by choosing the animal approach in choices they make early in the day and not allowing negative energy to start their minds and lead the day as it goes forward. People can learn not to hold onto the anger and frustrations they may experience in accomplishing the need to work for food and shelter. They can prove to be much kinder by just living in the moment. That is how the animal kingdom chooses to survive and without this beautiful instinct, not much would be in existence at this time.

So as you see, man is given choices for a path that can serve him and it is not too late to move forward in a better way. Making a choice to share goodness is part of the nourishment of the soul every day. This can bring a body into a place of contentment, love, and honor. We will help in any way it is chosen by man, if asked. One has many choices ahead and each action at this time shall ring true to the soul's readiness to make the right decisions based on life at this time.

Earth Transitions

This piece of their book is very special to me, as it talks about simple actions that we can take to make huge changes for all who inhabit our Earth. "Grace" and "gratitude" seem to be the buzz words that are trending today and when you really accept in your heart these wonderful tools, they do change your life.

I have had the opportunity to be the recipient of getting to know grace when I was feeling lost and frustrated from curveballs we get at certain learning times in our lives. Grace picked me up, stood me straight up and allowed me to pass the test of those challenges, and I have been rewarded for accepting the changes they brought and being grateful for the lessons they gave me. Today grace is part of my life toolbox right up there with manners and integrity. It certainly showed me the way to understand gratitude and feel the greatness of speaking my appreciation many times a day.

I really spend a lot of time talking to my clients about giving to others and how we benefit from it. One of the quickest ways to feel emotionally good about yourself is to follow some of the information written by these wonderful beings. It can be addicting when you get the first benefit handed to your heart, just from doing a special deed. Clients come back to tell me how this new way of thinking has changed their lives and has brought them so much peace and understanding. Giving and receiving has multiplied the amount of love they can share so much more freely with the world today and this changes Earth's energy every moment, one molecule at a time.

* * * * *

We are here tonight to talk about the Earth's transitions at this time. Man plays a key role in what the outcome shall be for all. You will play a part in the security of mankind which we know today is ever-changing. How, you ask, can one small soul play a part in bringing Earth back into balance? Collectively, we are together if we desire to participate. Again, it's about free will without any gain for ourselves on an individual basis. We all have a predetermined job in keeping this world on track and stable for all men, women, and children for generations to come. Negative discussions are operating at a very high level and it is up to you to change the direction of the unhealthy energy flowing and collecting into great blobs that are not good for man.

You may ask how you can change this feeling of loss of love and grace for each other. The job each of you holds at this time is to be building blocks of positive energy to create a solid platform of love and balance flowing freely and avoid the destruction that is upon you at this time.

We speak of loving kindness and compassionate grace and many consider them words for the New Age. Not to be, we say – they are words for now. Starting small when our feet hit the floor for morning rituals, let this be a time to reflect on how you are preparing to start your day. It only takes a moment to pray words of gratitude and offer help to all who come your way today. Whether it is to open a car door, hand a grocery cart to someone before you take one for yourself, or give another a sense of recognition that they count and just be kind. The flow of energy in the other person's body changes rapidly and then another gesture from them can be as simple as picking up a misplaced piece of trash that has fallen from a vehicle. This makes the street a prettier walk and includes the bonus of not feeling as much anxiety as you hurry along, maybe otherwise missing the blooming flowers and beautiful white clouds floating in the blue sky. To miss these in the moment of every day is not part of God's plan.

Respect your Earth and that what it provides for you is there for the taking. This can happen by one small act that grows in many ways if you will take the time to start the flow. Lending a hand or a smile to another can increase your life in years as well theirs. Kindness can elevate the desire to do good things for others and make the world a better place. You will feel the love multiplying within you, as it becomes a permanent part of your daily life.

Love comes to us in such small ways that man has forgotten the creation of goodness from others; watch for this. Take the time out of your day to be aware of the value of this energy; give others a smile and greet them with joy. You will find you are the recipient of the same joy and find your step will be higher and your heart will be lighter. What a wonderful plan to make for yourself every day.

IN CONCLUSION

Every moment has value for each of you. There is only one moment that shall exist at any time and that is the only one to focus on; it is unique to the one behind and most certainly the one ahead. Know that each cell of your body reacts with only the present moment as the one you need, and once passed it shall be gone forever. It should also be understood that all you really have for accountability is not the moment, but the value in the moment and how you may use it for yourself or others.

It is up to you to determine which way you choose to live at any time. How you greet your day is your temperature for mindful ideas available to you; your actions are based on this temperature at the moment the information comes into your energy field. Choose how you treat others and you will find that you will lean more toward a tendency to do good deeds.

Not all will find this shift easy, as there has been a very long process of living in a negative space of not feeling that kindness is important. Change is going to be hard and will test all humans who feel the need to make a difference. There is a divine intervention upon all of you; understand, each of you souls will represent a beacon. Every thought, word and action becomes real the minute it is spoken and released.

Looking Ahead

This story is about a woman I knew through another client, whose reading had answered some questions about a friend she was very concerned for, as so much of the young woman's life had been spent in deep negativity. The woman in question, Crystal, had grown up in a small town, with both parents alcoholic and both siblings also carrying the gene for alcohol addiction. Today her brothers are without homes, living off social security while they continue street lives of alcohol and drug use.

When the call came in, I could tell had many questions regarding her path starting into her second year of college and how the next few years would go. It had been a struggle for Crystal to continue schooling and function in life without much human support. She was studying for a nursing degree and, as hard as it had been with so many monumental obstacles, she just knew finishing her schooling would mean being able to help others and become the person she had always wanted to be. She was feeling the pull of a life path every day to continue to move forward no matter how hard it was and wanted to believe there was a chance to make a difference in other's lives, that there was more than life as she had lived it.

With all of the problems at hand, Crystal didn't seem to have the constitution to pull it off. Her low grades were coming from working a full-time job on top of finding time for school and being in an abusive relationship with yet another alcoholic male. She knew the relationship was coming to an end and it was time to move on, so the pain from all of the issues growing up and then having another dysfunctional relationship was on her mind every waking moment.

I asked if she had thought about trying meditation to help with anxiety, and was pleased to hear she had just started attending a group and was feeling some success with the practice. I explained the need to think about the words and thoughts she was creating in her life which were so negative that she was prophesying a life of unhappiness and losing the will power to make the changes she needed. Crystal had a very hard time understanding the human ability of foretelling their lives. How could this happen with just saying a few words of negativity? Well, she got an earful on the need to speak words of kindness, gratitude, and love!

You deserve good words coming from yourself every day regardless of the path you have chosen. Remember one thing, one simple thing – you are God's creation and he gives you the power to take your life to the next level. Gratitude increases the energy level in your body; it stimulates your mind and nourishes your soul; it increases your joy and then that energy works overtime with each smile and act of kindness you share with another human. She got quiet for a few minutes and said she might have the ability to make some changes. Even though she did not feel like it was the answer, she still wanted to know love was going to be in her life.

She needed the company of positive affirmations speaking to her on a daily basis; I explained that even written words have life and energy. Especially important are the ones you choose to make upon awakening, so I told her to speak this affirmation out loud every morning and night: "I truly love myself and I am grateful to have this life to grow into the great spiritual being I want to be." These few words are absolutely contagious, and before long you will be saying them more than twice a day. You will feel your heart chakra rotate when you speak these powerful words. Just remember, you are what you speak. Your body can be healed of emotions and actions not worthy of who you are. I had no doubt Crystal was destined to find the love of her life with only a small change in her belief system, knowing that she was worthy of the right man and she had something valuable to bring to the relationship – herself.

At the end of the reading, she was much calmer. I knew it would take time to get herself into the groove of believing she had the ability to heal herself and make positive changes to create a life of love and kindness with a special person. No question, Crystal was destined to rub shoulders with a Soldier of Kindness, as they are always present to assist you when you evoke the desire to know love and share kindness from heart to hand.

I feel in my heart that she will circle back around to make a call to me and I look forward to that day, as I know she will be in the best spot ever for her life with her perfect mate.

* * * * *

It is easy to talk of changes and they will come in due time for man to see results and then there shall come a much more attractive way of life for all who take the time to feel love and practice it. Not all will find this shift easy as there has been a very long process of living in a negative space of not feeling that kindness is important. Many ask "Why?" That is the exact word to send off a signal to bypass the work that is invaluable for change, like taking time away from personal desires and other things.

Change is going to be hard and will test all humans who feel the need to make a difference. For this, you have to see a divine intervention is upon all of you. It is brought up in the mind so many times for you to finally buy into the real possibility that you are being guided to a new way of thought and should trust the process. This knowing will begin the change and walk you through many "aha" moments in your growth to understand the need for kindness which will breathe through every cell within your body and every mental capacity. There will not be a walk down the street or past a desk at work that this new life you will experience will not emit this lovely energy. Much will be broken down and new faces that you have passed by will now be upon you and be part of your life in goodness and grace.

Kindness will make you healthy in ways not quite seen in the medical world today. There are experiments that are being conducted now that will eventually be made available by a Soldier of Kindness. Through the kind work of this high entity, there will be facilitators in the medical industry to search for procedures that man can undertake at this time to improve health and live longer in the body's new, kind state. The act of simple kindness shall bring diseases to their knees, do away with many medicines, and help others besides yourself in the process.

Of course, all souls face bodily strain, can ordain sickness, and may put suffering out for those that will partake in this destruction if it is their desire. Stress is one of those evil outcomes of being a negative soul and choosing not to create a life of health. There is a plan you see with each Soldier to create the best energy for this world to experience, to show that wars and violence are not needed, not only around the world but in everyday homes right here and now as we speak.

You will see more of this kindness connection to physical health throughout the next few years. Man will return to historic ways of living and uncomplicate the soul's temple. To not have the fear of death upon you, after the golden years reach you, will be a blessing for many who want to stay active and feel they still have more to give to this world. Understand, each of you souls will represent a beacon.

Living Your Moments

Living in the moment can be hard to practice and takes a tremendous amount of time to become proficient at as a daily way of living. Certainly, to cut out all of the white noise and bad habits is a daunting task for the best of us. The reading I am going to talk about here not only had an effect on my client, but I also received a little bonus for myself.

I received the call one morning out of the blue and could tell Jackie was experiencing overwhelming stress, not just trying to stay grounded in her everyday life, but also about to take on a summer job as a yoga instructor. She had the experience but had left her practice a few years earlier to backpack throughout Alaska.

The trip had proved to be a tough adjustment, as she and her boyfriend were gone for 16 months working fishing boats. She wanted to learn the ropes, so to speak, but ended up as an extra hand in the large boat's food service, learning to cook for the 60-plus hungry workers on board. What proved to be a hard job, and having spent so much time in survival mode, were more than Jackie wanted to admit. The fast pace and daunting task of staying upright on rough seas had taken its toll and the breakup of her relationship was the final straw. Coming home was a blessing and a curse for her, as she was not prepared for the emotional roller coaster and lack of focus.

The reading was not indicating she would fill her days with downward-dog yoga poses, but that there was more water in her future, actually very warm water. I began to lay out her potential new life as a culinary student working in Florida for a large resort. No question, she was headed for a calmer environment than her last adventure. We talked about the spiritual path Jackie was beginning to see for herself and I recommended a class in meditation to help her reach a state of peace and calmness. She had practiced a simple meditation with her yoga but left it behind because of her inability to gain traction, as she said, and felt it was not helpful for her. As I have said, I am not a doctor and refuse to play one, yet having scanned her situation I felt she needed to be checked out for any health conditions that may be lingering, so I asked if she had been diagnosed for any attention deficit conditions. In fact, she had experienced this challenge when she was in grammar school and refused to take her medication! She promised that a trip to the doctor would be her next step.

We continued to talk about the need for a meditation class and spending a few minutes each day writing down her thoughts after each meditation, then waiting a few weeks to read the journal she would be creating. I also asked her to make a list of what she would like to accomplish in the next two years, wait- three days to look at the notes and remove the items that didn't spark a feeling of excitement or inspiration, then note the remaining few and give me a call; she still had a lot more work to accomplish. As a final reminder at the end of our call, I asked her to check out the culinary school vision I had and add it to her list.

One month after our original reading, I received a call from Jackie and she was much calmer. She had seen the doctor who confirmed she had an attention deficient issue and was placed on some meds that were working. She was also excited to tell me she had checked out local culinary schools and found one that had a very high rate of employment for their students and was ready to enroll. And she had started a meditation class with a spiritual group which met once a week.

Her daily journaling was a great success, as Jackie was learning so much about herself in the process. One special gift buried in her journaling was her desire to write poetry. She was finding so much peace and softness in her ability to find meaning when she spent time in nature and let herself experience words like raw, beautiful music as she honored living in the moment of God's wonder.

More recently we reconnected and she sent a video of some vegetarian recipes she had put together for me – isn't that a bonus! Jackie is now working in the Caribbean Islands for a beautiful, small resort, enjoying the sunsets and taking in the wonderful moments of life in the now.

* * * * *

Every moment has value for each of you. Understanding the importance of each instant is a process that man shall develop over time, which shall start from the first inhalation of life and shall continue until there is no breath left in the body. There is a large amount of information that each soul must filter to get the nuggets that are needed to take the next step forward and leave behind the moments that have passed.

Understand, there is only one moment that shall exist at any time and that is the only one to focus on. There shall be no value in the moments passed, as they have no value in your present; they shall not hold the same sounds or motions you may see at the current time. Every moment is unique to the one behind and most certainly the one ahead. And should you attempt to think of the moment ahead, you shall miss the immediate, important feeling, emotion, and knowledge that the universe has placed in your hands to fill your brain, eyes, heart, and all the cells of your body with pure awe and love for the presence of God.

Know that each cell of your body reacts with only the present moment as the one you need, and once passed it shall be gone forever. If you are creating a negative moment from the past, this shall be the time to set it free, simply allow it to filter out of the mind, and not let it affect the present moment. Realize you have the power to change and cure sickness in each moment of breath and awareness. Thinking of a future moment can bring positive or negative energy, depending on how you are accepting the current moment you are involved with and understanding it is the most important one for your body right at the time.

Think of a time when you have had a moment of anger and you allowed it to last for several minutes, moving negativity into your future just by continuing to think of something from the past. You actually changed how your cells were instructing your organs to operate for those minutes. It does not take long for an artery to suffer damage or a wrong move of your legs to bring a fall. This can happen in a short moment, and then you say "If I had only paid attention to what I was doing just now!"

There is a lesson to learn from not being present at the time of injuries and bad decisions, as an instance of time that can never be gained back; there is no do-over. Every moment is attached to an action that you can use and gain value from when you have moved on, as it shall never be repeated again. It may seem to be a senseless action to want to remember the value of living your moments but recognize how valuable you can find them, as none shall be wasted in idle awareness.

It should be understood all you really have for accountability is not the moment but the value in the moment and how you may use it for yourself or others. This is a time to view the health of the body and how important it is to manage actions of anger, fear, appreciation, and happiness. Show gratitude to your body and its well-being, as this can affect your work and personal relationships, and these deserve your attention at the appropriate time.

Living in the moment means that you are completely aware of how your world is working around you at this time and the effect of your presence in it. You can and will understand the need for calmness as you grow in this new awareness. Everything around you shall have meaning and allows you to receive the answers to optimize your own existence by how you may choose to act at this instant to all that is surrounding you.

The world is a place of imperfections if you live in the commonplace understanding of how the world is currently spinning at this time. But shall you decide to stay in the moment then you will become aware of the perfection that is shining brightly all around you. The world that surrounds you can resonate in sync with your cells just the same as it does with all creatures that share this beautiful Earth. With greater awareness, every moment shall give you peace, and appreciation of your life will reflect in the moments you remember, not the moments you have lost.

Mindfulness and Managing Karma

This writing touches back on the importance of being accountable for our thoughts, and so I believe it serves well as the final piece. As you have seen throughout this book, our thoughts are so powerful that they can literally change the direction not only of our physical health but our life-path contracts. This is exactly what Peter and his non-physical friends wanted to communicate to us when all of this was channeled.

I have two things to share in my section here. First is my own experience with mindfulness. It shows the power of thoughts and how negativity can overtake a life, actually mine, and how a compelling message from a higher power came to me from a total stranger. Second is a reading that supports my belief in karma, and emphasizes how powerful it is for all of us to realize the responsibility we have to each other and find the paths to our own loving consciousness through free will. It is powerful and thought-provoking to consider how we can lose ourselves on a daily basis if we are not spending time each day to fill our hearts with forgiveness and embrace a sincere love for ourselves.

A few years ago I was going through a rough patch of health issues and found myself just a little depressed. Now mind you, I am a very happy person and pride myself on my laugh and ability to find good in most things. So being even a little depressed certainly was not my style nor was it a place I wanted to spend very long visiting. Once I became aware of my plight, I noticed in a simple conversation with a total stranger that my attitude was full of negative comments and walked away feeling poorly about myself. Needless to say, I went straight home and made a list of all of the negative thoughts I was harboring at that time and I was astonished to see how long the list was.

I immediately went to work to create a second column of positive thoughts to counteract the negative ones. I made an affirmation for every thought as it came into my day and in less than 24 hours, I was writing nothing but a long list of good thoughts and actions. A few days later my back pain was getting better, I felt good again, and my laugh had returned in full force. It was a great awakening for me to live my life with greater mindfulness and purpose every day, and the outcome has been a game changer for me – daily gratitude.

Every evening now I have a small ritual to check for any negative thoughts I may have internalized during the day, close my eyes and gather them all up, then send them to an open portal in the universe to remove them from my energy field and my mind, replacing them with good thoughts of the coming morning and the intention to acknowledge them upon waking. Now, it may seem like a big nuisance to spend so much time on this, but I will tell you I am a happy camper and will work hard to interact with strangers, giving at least one complement each morning. I get more out of the kind words than the person I choose to bestow them upon. I know I am able to create my destiny with my thoughts and it is has a direct influence on how I feel physically and mentally.

Secondly, the reading I want to share with you is about a client who felt broken when she called me for direction and *understanding about why she couldn't forgive her father for his abuse of her mom, her sister, and herself. Karen had grown up in daily fear of her mother being beaten and if she or her sister intervened then they too would suffer at his hand. Due to the severity of the beatings, her mother passed away. Social services immediately removed her and her sister, placing them in separate foster homes until they reached 18 years of age. She spoke of having wanted every single day, for the past 20 years, to kill her father for the painful loss of her mother and the violent memories she experienced.*

Although her younger sister went on to college, married, and was a successful nurse manager for a hospital in another state, they didn't stay in touch with one another. Karen spoke of her own drug use, trying to block out the abusive years and overcome her guilt for what happened to her mother. She talked about finding her father's apartment while under the influence of drugs and sitting outside planning to kill him. This was a daily desire, thinking if she completed it then she could be free. Although she never followed through, she had spent most of her adult life planning revenge for what had happened to her family.

Finally, sick and broken from the abuse of drugs and alcohol, Karen wanted to be free and clean to live out the rest of her life without the guilt of her mom's death. During the reading, we talked about how focusing on revenge for so many years was holding her back, allowing karma to take over her body and take away her life. Still, she wanted the karma to be felt by her father for all he had afflicted on the family and rightfully so. I explained to her that he would and probably already was experiencing the result of karma even as we spoke. Certainly a carryover from a past life could have been playing out for both of them at that time.

When we were close to finishing the reading, I asked her to get a piece a paper and write about forgiving her father's abuse and the loss of her mother at his hands. Then to write another paper forgiving herself for what she had carried for so many years and the abuse she had caused her own body, mind, and spirit. I asked her to get two helium balloons of whatever design and color she was attracted to, then find a place where she felt safe and comfortable to complete her ritual once she had prepared her written notes.

Karen found her favorite place at the beach and tied the notes to each balloon, stood there for a moment in contemplation, and prepared to release them one at a time. For each balloon, she paid attention to the energy in the soles of her feet and allowed that energy to flow up into her body until it reached the top of her head. And when she felt it was right, she released the balloon with its notes and acknowledged the release of her anger, watching it float out of her life forever, and felt the rise of her forgiveness. When she was ready to leave, she just turned around without looking back as she got in her car and drove away. Karen now had the opportunity to live in a new and profound way that meant having the freedom to take her life back.

I heard from her one year to the date of her balloon release for another reading, sober and clean. She had been visiting her sister out west, was going to art school, and was teaching painting classes to abused kids. Her last words to me that day were crystal clear of her love for herself and wanting to be of service to help others overcome their abused past. Karen had finally found her place in life and felt at peace for the first time in many years.

Thank you to my non-physical friends for the reminder of how important it is to take responsibility for our thoughts and actions. May we all be open to receiving help and messages from a higher power, however they come into our lives. And may we all come to love the opportunity to grant goodness to others every day, knowing it creates a chain reaction. I do hope you will find a message here that can bring your heart to your hand.

* * * * *

How you greet your day is your temperature for mindful ideas available to you. Information is currently floating around in the atmosphere and is there for the taking by anyone that has opened themself to it. Yet your actions are based on your temperature at the moment the information comes into your energy field. This is why any humans can experience road rage and depression, or enhance their creative skills, simply from the mindset they are carrying.

Information comes to us on a constant basis, to assimilate and decide energetically whether it fits into our mental bank of ideas and desires. When it is positive, there is a very powerful action that can soothe the muscles and set the cells of the body to work at full speed. Mindfulness creates an opportunity to better receive information that you desire, depending on the energy held in the mind and body at that time, whereas the continual path of a careless lifestyle will build up an attitude of indifference – those are the ones blocking energy until they can no longer see the sun for its beauty.

Every thought, word, and action becomes real the minute it is spoken and released. This is why all humans should be very careful with the information they emit into the atmosphere at all times. Negativity is abundant and it should become your responsibility to keep this energy in check. Karma comes every second for each of you – meaning a trade-off, if you remember the rule. Karma is not something of need; it is a matter of choice and free will. Your karma is based upon good and not-so-good deeds that you complete throughout the day.

It is up to you to determine which way you choose to live at any time. As your day goes, you are creating positive karma from a good deed to anyone, even the Earth. Negative karma that you create can come from something as simple as a mean thought toward someone, or an unkind word. Words can be harmful and the body reacts poorly when you keep repeating them in the mind. Many words that you use are hard to swallow, causing energetic pain, and the path of these words rolling around in your brain leads to deterioration. Negative words can cause your organs to dry out and not feel warm and nourished; the brain can shrink as it dies from the lack of restorative reasoning. It can also spark good health from positive thoughts. It is up to man at this time to think how thoughts and words can harm or support all aspects of a soul's existence.

Choose how you treat others and you will find that you will lean more toward a tendency to do good deeds.

This choosing can be some of the karmic debt you are completing from other lives. Negative karmic debt can be carried through many lifetimes and weighs heavily on your soul, as well as giving rise to the body's breakdown. Reincarnation allows you to reenact what you have brought forth from a previous life, to repeat the same way or to make amends that will offer personal growth and spiritual elevation. Give up anger and revenge, no matter how hard you want to seek others' pain. Remember to forgive and to release any desire for revenge at this time and always; you will receive no bad karma for this.

Always give negative feelings up to God and he will grace you with goodness. Allow others to do as they desire in using their own free will, as they also have a choice to create good or bad karma. Take time in your morning and at night to propose a life of joy, peace, and a promise to be of service to someone you meet along your path each day. Take the time to feel the wind blow and stop to notice how God graces your cheek with his hands at that time. Do we really need to see it to feel it? The answer to this is NO; God shows you many ways to feel Him in every part of your lives. You may feel His warm caress on your hand through an angel or from a small tickle on your arm. Know that you are touched by many in this body you have, and remember how much love and support you have around you at all times.

We thank you for your heart and hand.

PETER'S RECOMMENDATIONS

Peter and his non-physical friends have chosen some daily exercises based on the material in this book to assist you in your daily life. I hope you find these useful on your journey of greater mindfulness, deeper spiritual growth, and better health. This book repeatedly emphasizes joy, kindness, compassion, and the need to attain a higher vibration to align yourself with love for yourself and others in our world. Peter speaks here again of the need for meditation, breath, and stillness to elevate our spiritual mind, body, and soul -- all useful in any of the writings.

Certainly, there are many forms of meditation and for those both new and experienced in following a heightened spiritual path, this information will serve as an introduction to and a confirmation of such practices. The astral authors desired that you be able read any section of this book and never be lost; they also intend that these recommendations will work the same way, so find what is needed and resonates with you.

Morning Stretch

Before rising in the morning, stretch your body by extending the legs and arms and hold for 10 seconds, and turning your head side-to-side three times. Lie still for a few moments and pay attention to the rhythm of your breathing, taking deep breaths until you feel you have filled your heart with all the love the universe has to offer. Envision your heart vibrating love for all who may come into contact with you during your day and looking into their eyes and gifting them with a smile. Although you may miss your exercise a few times, you will soon be smiling straight from your heart to everyone without the mindful thoughts you started out with. It is at this time you will feel the love you have just received from always keeping your heart full of the energy of pure love; you will have received the gift of your efforts for Goodness and Grace.

Morning Light From Heaven

Begin everyday with mindful love for the new day. Lie quietly, close your eyes, and envision a light gracing your body, swirling inside your heart. Continue to watch the light grow larger until your body is awash in this light extending beyond your energy field. Imagine as you go through this process, you are cleansing any negative energy or debris that has been held in the body overnight. Intend in prayer to be able to offer those you come into contact with today the opportunity to change a broken moment in their lives. This process shall send out clean energy as you move through your day. Understand you are sharing a light from the heavens and creating a calmness around you that others can take into their own energy fields bringing some lightness for them to experience in their day.

Morning Gratitude

Every morning when you awake, you must realize what God has just gifted you with. Spend a few moments to speak your gratefulness to elevate your energy. Imagine a day of God's light shining for you and around you at all times; imagine another day to share your good graces and health with total strangers and be grateful to know the light is for you to use at your discretion. Remind someone of how grateful you are to have met them or to have them in your life. Make a point to express your gratefulness 10 times a day, through some type of contact and voice your words out loud. You will change the energy everywhere you have been and shall leave a trail of light behind you for others to follow.

Meditation

Meditation is a positive tool for any spiritual quest. Sitting in silence can be the beginning of this tool for your connections. You will find this practice can help you grow and open a deeper connection. There can be much said for any human to choose to venture into this practice with other like-minded individuals. The opportunity to connect at a higher vibration is valid in groups and experiences shared can assist you to connect with a more mindful participation. If you are concerned about not being able to sit in silence, then use a guided tape of your choosing.

Breathing

Place both feet on the floor, close your eyes, and take a deep breath through the nose; hold it for five seconds and then blow it out through your mouth, as you imagine you are creating a vortex within the lungs, pulling out the toxins and negativity that has lain dormant there. Continue your exhale until you are completely spent of air, unable to push any more air from your lungs. Breathe at your natural pace for 30 seconds before you do this again, allowing the body a small rest for the lungs to slowly adjust to this new way of breathing. This time can shrink as your lungs gain their spiritual strength. Repeat the exercise five times total. Sit in silence and imagine your lungs are clean, pink in color, and healthy, filling up with perfect energy for each new breath to continue. This exercise can be done as needed or may become part of your daily practice. It can become a natural cleansing of the body through the learned strength you have created for the lungs and muscles needed to perform this exercise.

Sitting In Silence

Calm your energy, take some deep breaths, and sit in stillness as you wait for the silence to speak to you; use this time to ask for messages that will benefit you. It may take a few tries for you to begin receiving information and it will not always come in silence. Should you have a strong feeling, act upon it, and trust in what you hear. Say "thank you" for the presence of non-physical guides and their teachings.

Contacting Guides

Sit in stillness at least five minutes for this silence. It is best to come with a thought of you want to work on with your non-physical guides; ask the question and utilize the silence to listen for the answer, which will come when the time is right for you in your growth. Have faith in what you receive when you ask the questions; we are available for you and it is best to use your faith in trusting the answers. Be more open to any signs that feel legitimate and you will increase the ability to have a strong connection. It is available to you all times; you need to wait and listen. This could take a while; you have to allow it to come to you and then choose to stay on your path.

Looking For Messages

Look around your surroundings, TV programs, newspapers – even a complete stranger engaging you in conversation may offer you a message that fits directly with what you are looking for. The more you use this method to have contact, the better you will understand how easy the connection can be. Ask for help, expect results, and say "thank you." Your guides are very happy to know their hard work is getting through to you and will make the flow faster and easier for you to understand.

Listening For Messages

Sit in stillness each day for a small amount of time; calm your body's energy and imagine you are opening a pipeline of information to be processed and made useful to you. It shall be your choice of morning or evening for you to honor the presence of your guides but it would be helpful to sit the same time each day if possible. Trust in this channel of knowledge and pay attention to the strong emotions that come forward or cycles of thought around information, then act accordingly. Listen to the inner questions you are processing at all times and expect answers, as this shows your faith that you will trust the authenticity of what you receive. Remember to act on the information your guides provide you. You will find the channel will get better in time and they will appreciate the trust you are exhibiting in their assistance.

Rituals

Rituals can be reading the paper before you shower with your morning coffee or doing crossword puzzles on the train to work. They all count for some desired outcome to comfort or expand your skills. This is good. We would like to impart rituals that can help you heal from health issues, clean up negativity surrounding you, or improve your reaction to your daily life. Take a few minutes before you leave your home in the morning and voice your gratitude for this new day with a joyful little dance and offer each person you come in personal contact with during the day a smile and a verbal "hello." You have just increased your own vibration and in each moment of grace that you show someone, they will feel the instant desire to show kindness to another. They may not even be sure where the instant moment of joyful love came from, but will keep that energetic rush as they continue sharing.

Overcoming Fear

Fear is a state of mind that you use as an excuse to not move forward with the unknown; it shall keep you from living the life you are here to experience. Spend a few moments in quiet stillness when this emotion starts to surface in you. Imagine the anxiety leaving your mind and the tension leaving your body as you breathe deeply, closing one nostril at a time; continue three times for each nostril and release. Envision darkness leaving your body opening your mind to the beauty of reaching the goals you set for yourself. Speak feelings of successfully reaching the positive outcome you are looking for and being free of all anxieties you may have harbored for yourself.

Preventing Anger

Anger is an emotion that can change the dynamics of the cells of your body in the blink of an eye and shall cause a misfire to the brain that blocks the arteries, killing cells and causing illness that can have life-altering effects. Go outside each morning before you get dressed for the day; stand on the Earth and feel your energy rising from the soles of your feet to the top of your head, grounding you and offering you the chance to locate and release any negativity you have collected. Should you have a habit of creating anxiety during your morning travel to work or errands, it is a good time for you to speak of your love for others – this will allow your day to begin with a higher level of safety. And as you travel, offer others your assistance to make others' day easier by allowing them a chance to move in front of you. Speak of safety for the sake of those you see driving in an unsafe way, understanding that they may be late or having a bad morning. Let it be clear that you intend your spoken words to directly reach those you are trying to help.

Prayer

Prayers are the highest form of contact that humans can make with God and love can create a vortex of energy that will envelop those you pray for. In preparation for your prayers, it is best to sit in silence for yourself and do a mindful cleansing of any negative energy from your body. Envision a golden light from the soles of your feet and pull this light up through your body, lifting out the debris and negative energy. Speak your prayer with assurance and faith in a positive outcome. Give thanks.

Helping Tired Eyes

Your eyes are the doorway to the soul and should they suffer from any obstacles of tiredness, burning, or feeling overused, it would be helpful to honor this direct pathway to the third eye with rest. Place a warm compress over the eyes for three minutes while lying quietly and envision all debris being removed from them, giving way to clear sight, and ask for the correct infused energy needed for the eyes to heal and operate at perfection. This needs to be done while lying down and in a resting position. This exercise should be used on a regular basis for the third eye to remain at its highest function at all times, accompanied by a short meditation with the focus for the third eye's health and vibration.

Heightening the Five Spiritual Body Senses

The connection for all of the body senses to work at their optimum cell health shall be to remove the negative energy surrounding you daily. The spiritual body operates on love, kindness and compassion. Each of the five senses are connecters to this guidance and each sense needs to operate in this positive way. It should be considered a part of your daily ritual to cleanse the body of negative energy and place an image of love, kindness, and compassion into the lungs of all who come into contact with you during your day. You are the acting ambassador for any Spiritual Sense to share with any souls in need of this assistance

Affirmations

The use of affirmations is going to be listed many times in our recommendations, as it is a sure provider of increasing your body's energy and elevating your goals every time you speak and see them. Affirmations should speak of who you want to become and deserve to be. They will affirm your faith for truth and that you will call to live in truth with their use. Sit quietly, find your vision of what you want in your life, and believe you will reach it. Write the desires you have and place them on your bathroom mirror; put them up as the background screen on your phone, iPad, computer – anywhere you are likely to see them during your day. Say them out loud; feel their energy; bring them alive with your speech and in your mind.

Helping Strangers

Make a list of five things you can do for total strangers every day. Open doors, give a compliment, allow someone to pull ahead of you in traffic, let someone be first in the grocery store, or pay for the coffee of the person behind you without telling them. Participate in giving love freely to another without any expectations. Spend a few moments in silence and ask the universe to grant you a loving non-physical being to assist you in finding and connecting with the right person who could use a special blessing. The time to trust your special helper to alert you may be as you are taking a walk in the park to catch up with someone that you feel could and would accept your company along the walk or sitting with someone and ask them how they are feeling. Follow your heart and give a compliment, or ask them questions that speak love and kindness towards them. It can be a wonderful way to spend your lunch or afternoon break. The one you have blessed may desire to share with another. The more the light you share, God will fill your heart with more. You will receive back far more than any of your gifts to others for such kind gestures.

Body Scan

Before bedtime, spend a few minutes to scan your body for any blocks you may be experiencing; this can be done by finding the block through joint pain or soreness. Take your first three fingers and massage the tissue in small circles proceeding to larger circles as you continue to massage, and at that time speak to the tissue of becoming smooth and healthy. Use this method on any area that has pain or soreness. Although you may not have diminished the pain, you will have started to infuse the tissue with the movement needed and the body's rest shall begin the healing process. This jumpstarts the cells of the body to release any fluid being held in the blocked area.

Love of Self

Love is the source of health for the human body; every cell depends on the bounty of love to grow and maintain its proper level of operation. Spend time in your morning cleansing ritual to verbally express the beauty of your body and appreciation for its strong bones and glowing skin, combining the miracle of structure and function. Imagine all the cells of your body operating at their highest level; see all foods you offer for the cells' growth to be of the highest nourishment, supporting the temple of the soul; offer your breath as fuel for cleansing and forming the oxygen needed to keep the cells moving for the good of the body. Spend time in nature to express your appreciation of plant life growing to offer its beauty to you and to create the immense energy that flows around you, keeping the air perfect for you to take in to your lungs. Do all of this for yourself and for all who call this Earth home.

Attitude

Embracing each day with an attitude of love, kindness, and joy shall keep the body in good health and the mind adjusted to good mental function. This can elevate another human with the same energy when you offer love without any bias or expectation. Make it a part of your daily ritual to offer kindness, love, and joy to another. Use free moments to find an aspect of goodness in any situation you face and allow this to grow without any thoughts of negativity.

Healing Thyself

Begin each day with a mindful desire to keep your body in the highest level of health. If you are not in this space at the time, spend time to inwardly reflect on any stress you may be experiencing and the cause of its condition; as we have spoken before, your body can heal itself by simply correcting the mind. Sit in stillness with silence and allow the body to catch up with the mind. This will offer you a clearer cell connection to provide the nerves a better current to operate throughout your body. Choose silence in stillness every day for at least five minutes upon rising and ending your day to increase your memory and allow the brain to grow new cells for optimum health. Adding this ritual to your morning and evening meditation with mindfulness to relieve the stress carried throughout the day will supply your body and mind with strong health benefits.

PETER'S EPILOGUE

For you who are reading these last few words, we hope you realize our desire has been to let all humans know we exist in all worlds and we are always ready to assist you in your life's journey. This book was written for those who choose a path of goodness and grace, seek to know God, and desire a life that helps all who call Earth home. Your Creator wants you to see yourselves and each other through His eyes and His love, that your world will not only survive but abound in love, kindness, compassion, peace, and patience, with God's Soldiers offering assistance to every man, woman, child, and creature alike. We have chosen to show you this path and hope you shall promote a life of love for any who come into your space.

Let it be understood, we are not leaving your presence at the end of this book, as we are only a word away from helping you grow into the great, loving soul that you desire to become. As you have read this material, there has been an ethereal thread attached to your being through the feelings and beliefs you are pondering, which shall grow in such a wondrous way for the betterment of you and everyone around you.

As we have spoken before, we have much to share with your world and we take this time to announce there shall be another book of our spoken words to help you have a better understanding of your purpose and direction as your season shall come to completion. God's Soldiers shall share their written work in a soul's journey home, revealing the very moments experienced at death, the pathway that leads home, and the life that greets you upon reaching the afterlife.

We choose to deliver this information so you will have no fear of death, only happiness to be among your cherished family and longtime friends, embracing the true love of God's spiritual world, and knowing there is always opportunity for soul growth on both sides. And for all who wish to experience other transitions and more seasons of loving work for their soul's enlightenment, it shall also show you the process of coming back to Earth as one of God's chosen six Soldiers of Love, Kindness, Compassion, Peace, Patience, and Grace – if you choose.

We look forward to this next body of work we will be bringing from our heart to your hands.

ABOUT THE AUTHOR

Margaret Selby is an internationally known clairvoyant medium who has read for individuals and businesses throughout the world for over 30 years. She owns Feng Shui Concepts, conducts commercial business and residential real estate clearings and blessings, and speaks across the country on the afterlife, intuition, and Feng Shui.

Email Address: Margaret@margaretselby.com
Website Address: www.margaretselby.com
Phone number to schedule readings with Margaret: 1-844-542-6809
Follow me on Facebook: Psychic Readings by Margaret Selby
Twitter: Margaret Selby   @margaret_selby

Manufactured by Amazon.ca
Bolton, ON

27396423R00182